The
British Saloon Car
Championship

(1958-1972)

*highlighting the Triple-Winning
Era of the Bevan & McGovern Imp*

Martyn Morgan Jones

The British Saloon Car Championship
(1958-1972)

highlighting the Triple-Winning Era of the Bevan & McGovern Imp

Martyn Morgan Jones

BOOKMARQUE
PUBLISHING

Minster Lovell & New Yatt • Oxfordshire

To Doris Bevan and in memory of George

First published September 2004

British Library Cataloguing in Publication Data
A catalogue record for this book is available from the British Library

ISBN 1-870519-62-0

LIMITED CASEBOUND EDITION
*This book is produced in an edition of no more than 500 numbered copies
in hardback of which this is copy*

No. 68 /500

Frontispiece:
Triple Champion Bill McGovern in the Bevan Imp

Set in 10.5pt on 12.5 pt Palatino
Typesetting and origination by Bookmarque Publishing
Printed on Arrow 100 gsm
Published by Bookmarque Publishing
Printed and bound in England by Antony Rowe Limited

Contents

Acknowledgements

T HERE are many people I would like to thank—without their help this book would not have been possible. I hope that I have remembered all those individuals or organisations who were so kind in helping me obtain information and photographs and for allowing me their valuable time, so I apologise if I have inadvertently missed anyone out.

Doris Bevan, Peter Bevan, John Rose, Carolyn Jones, Bill McGovern, Dave Matthews, Les Nash, Vince Woodman, Jonathan Buncombe, Richard Longman, Ray Calcutt, Melvyn Adams, Jack Sears, Frank Gardner, Jussi Kynsilehto, Timo Saaristo, Dave Hill, Lynne and Gordon Wellbelove, Alan Knight, Alan Ramsay, Royston Paskins, Vanna Skelley, Robin Human, Frank de Jong, Joan Unett, James Beckett, Mark Foster, Richard Bunyan and Ted Walker.

Also kind thanks to: *Autosport* • BARC • BRDC • BRSCC • Beaulieu Library • British Racing Mechanics Club • Castrol Archives • Ferret Fotographics • Ford Archives • The Imp Club and Stevenage Area Centre • LAT Photographic • *Motoring News* (now titled *Motorsport News*) • Peugeot Sport • Safety Devices.

Martyn Morgan Jones

Foreword by Jack Sears

I SAW my first saloon car race at Silverstone in 1950 and was immediately attracted to the idea of one day competing in this category. Saloon Car Racing (now known today as Touring Cars) was, and still is, hugely popular with race fans who can instantly recognise the different makes of car.

I started racing in 1950 but it was not until 1957 that I raced saloon cars. In 1960 my good friend Tommy Sopwith asked me to join the late Mike Parkes in his Equipe Endeavour team, driving a Jaguar Mk II in the British Saloon Car Championship, an association that lasted three years. During this time Mike Parkes worked for the Rootes Group and was the development engineer for the Hillman Imp. I remember him bringing one of these cars to my home for me to evaluate and we spent a happy day driving around the highways and byways of Norfolk.

Little did I think then that it would become such a successful saloon car racer, the Bevan Imp winning three consecutive championships due to the engineering skill of George Bevan and the driving skill of Bill McGovern. I am so delighted to have seen this combination in action many times.

Jack Sears puts the hammer down in this ex-1963 Le Mans Cobra at Brands Hatch on 11 July 1964. He took an incredible victory in this infamous 'black flag' Ilford Trophy race .

Norfolk • August 2004

Introduction

SINCE its inception, those involved with saloon car racing have worked tirelessly to raise its profile, and its status has risen from pauper to prince. It is driven by technology whilst at the same time it pushes technology forward. It has developed into a formula that has witnessed, and continues to witness, the skills of some of the finest drivers and utilises Britain's most prestigious circuits. It is a formula with a real presence and a wonderful pedigree; to some, myself included, it is 'the' formula. I love the technicality and pace of today's racing saloons but, for me, the glory years spanned the period from 1963 to 1973. Things seemed much simpler back then.

Formula Won

Almost six decades have passed since the forerunners of today's super saloons scrabbled off the starting grid. By the time the Bevan Imp appeared in 1970, saloon car racing was in the ascendancy and the British Saloon Car Championship was the ultimate 'tin-top' challenge. A number of major manufacturers were represented and it was quite normal to witness Formula One aces battling it out with talented privateers.

In the 1970s it was also possible for a hard-working and skilled privateer team to take the glory. Ordinary people, with ordinary cars and ordinary(ish) budgets could be competitive. When the skills of George Bevan, Bill McGovern and a tremendous support network were added to the equation, then anything was possible.

The Bevan Imp was nothing special. It was just a well-engineered car, driven by a very quick driver and run by a small, dedicated and incredibly hard-working team. Indeed, it is fair to say that the Bevan Imp was probably one of the most 'standard' cars in the Championship and its mechanical specification could have been replicated by anyone should they have so desired. In my youth, I ran similar specification cars on the road—everyday!

I simply needed to write this account of the British Saloon Car Championship highlighting the 1970-72 era before it is forgotten. I admit that the class structure benefited the Imp (and other giant-killing small capacity cars over the years) and there is no doubt that this helped it get where it did, but read the story, check the lap times, peruse the overall positions and then make your own conclusion.

Martyn Morgan Jones
Grosmont, Wales • August 2004

CHAPTER 1

Racing Start

FOLLOWING the war just about every commodity was in short supply, and it would take years for Britain to get back on its feet. The motor industry, recovering from war work, was amongst the hardest hit. Petrol rationing would remain in operation for some time, there was prohibitive purchase tax on new cars, and raw material for the motor industry was in scarce supply.

Inevitably, when faced with these hurdles most manufacturers struggled. Many went through a period of consolidation and concentrated their energies on building mundane, medium-sized saloon cars. Nevertheless, there were a few exceptions—notably, the advanced Morris Minor, the multi-talented Land Rover and the lithe and potent Jaguar XK120.

It was some time before the status quo that existed before the war was restored. The keyword was survival; sports cars were generally perceived to be extravagant items and, on the whole, had a low priority. Bentley switched to the production of luxury cars and Alvis, well-known for its sports models, now concentrated on everyday tourers. For a while, Talbot, Singer and Sunbeam ignored the sporting market—and at Invicta, a company renowned for its sports cars, production almost ground to a halt.

Adversity can, however, be a great motivator and there was the odd glimpse of a silver living in the otherwise heavily laden skies. After its enforced hiatus, motor sport began to revive, largely because the now redundant airfields were proving to be ideal venues for competitive motoring.

1948 was something of a pivotal year—Goodwood opened its racing circuit, Silverstone ran its first Grand Prix, and thanks to a number of far-sighted individuals, saloon (or production, as it was then known) car racing began. These forward-thinkers appreciated that 'souping-up' and racing a family car could be cost-effective, fun, and something the public would have a great affinity with.

Starting Grid

Enthusiasm is one thing, but flights of fancy will only become reality if they are backed up by good organisation. Production car racing's early years were rather confused and poorly focused—saloon cars were forced to compete against sports cars—there was no specific category for either type. Thankfully, by the early 1950s, the situation had improved and the perception of saloon cars in racing was changing—until this time, saloon cars had been synonymous only with rallying.

Spearheading this movement was the BRDC (British Racing Drivers Club), which was involved mainly with racing at Silverstone, but also at other notable venues such as Brands Hatch.

Opposite page and above: sequence shows how A105 loses it but the lucky driver walked away …just!

In 1952, the *Daily Express* (effectively the BRDC's media partner), set a precedent by organising a very successful 'saloon-car-only' race at Silverstone. Before long separate classes for saloon cars became the norm, and by the mid-1950s Silverstone's race-goers had become accustomed to the sight and sound of tuned Consuls, Zephyrs, A90s, Jaguars, Rileys being driven on the ragged edge—and occasionally over it!

Right up until the late 1950s, the partnership of the BRDC and the *Daily Express* helped catalyse interest in, and focus attention on, saloon car racing in Britain.

Win on Sunday—Sell on Monday

Manufacturers (particularly Ford and BMC) began to wake up and smell the Castrol 'R'! Sporting marques such as Riley, Jaguar and MG started fielding teams of cars, and when drivers of the calibre of Ken Wharton, Mike Hawthorn and Stirling Moss slid into the driving seats, the enthusiasts really began to sit up and take notice. Soon, ever more sizeable crowds were making their way to Silverstone, keen to watch the slip-sliding action.

From being one of motor racing's lower echelons, this emergent category soon became an established part of the racing calendar and grew to be a firm favourite with competitors and spectators alike. But despite bucket loads of enthusiasm and plenty of on-track activity, saloon car racing was still without a 'proper' championship. Thankfully, behind the scenes, the stage was being set for what was effectively the forerunner of today's Touring Car Championship.

Racing Ahead

The BRSCC (British Racing & Sports Car Club), who had been observing the developments in saloon car racing, liked what it saw and acted. In 1958, building upon the BRDC's pioneering efforts, the BRSCC launched a full-blown and multi-venue British Saloon Car Championship—if you discounted the fact that six rounds were held at its main circuit, Brands Hatch! The racing was split into four separate classes: •Up to 1200 cc •1201-1600 cc •1601-2700 cc •2701 cc and over.

No exotic or outlandish modifications were allowed. Cars had to be standard catalogued four-seater saloons, of which at least 500 had to have been made. Straightforward alterations—for example, head polishing and the fitment of anti-roll bars—were allowed, but the standard tyre size had to be retained and power-improving double-choke carburettors were barred.

Race to the Finish

The first National Saloon Car Championship proved to be a resounding success attracting cars as diverse as Jaguars, Ford Zephyrs, Volvo Amazons, MG Magnettes, Ford Prefects, Austin A35s, Riley 1.5s, even Borgward Isabellas! The contest was a nail-biting affair and went right down to the wire. Incredibly, the result was a points draw between Tommy Sopwith in a Jaguar 3.4 and Jack Sears in his Austin A105 Westminster.

But championships, especially inaugural ones, need an outright winner. BMC's competition manager, Marcus Chambers, saved the day—he provided two identical Riley 1.5s, in which the drivers raced in two challenge races at Brands Hatch. In rain-lashed conditions the duellists splashed away from the start line. Sopwith, who had pole for the first race, held the lead coming home 2.2 seconds ahead of Sears. To ensure fair play, they swapped cars for the second race and set off into the murky distance once more. This time it was Sears who triumphed. He expertly steered his car around the waterlogged track, coming home 3.8 seconds in front—and by a mere 1.6 seconds on aggregate he became Champion.

Jack Sears (ahead in his A105) and Tommy Sopwith (3.4 Jaguar) close racing right to the end.

*The Bonneville Trophy
for the inaugural
National Saloon Car Championship.*

Championship Overhaul

For the following year the Championship ran to the FIA Appendix J Category C regulations and was won by Jeff Uren in a Ford Zephyr. In 1960 the series ran to 'SupaTura' format, where just about any modification was now possible and the Championship win went to Doc Shepherd and his Don Moore-prepared Austin A40.

From 1961 through to the end of 1965 FIA Group 2 regulations were adopted and as a result, saloon car racing experienced a much-welcomed period of stability. These regulations demanded minimum production runs and stipulated that engine and body modifications could only be undertaken if they were the same as those available on retail sale. Why was this so noteworthy? Well, it was only two years earlier that the Mini arrived on the scene!

This triumph of engineering and packaging went on to become one of the most significant cars of the twentieth century. Nippy, and extremely nimble, the Mini's 'performance' potential was obvious to many. BMC used the car to good effect and enjoyed Championship wins in 1961 with a Mini Minor and in 1962 with the hotter Mini Cooper. Variations on the Mini theme would go on to achieve more class and championship successes throughout the years.

Castrol Advert of November 1958.

The Mini arrives!

Jean Denton would go on to drive Imps. Here, though, she puts an early Mini Cooper through its paces.

BMC was now in pole position. Ford on the other hand was left languishing further down the grid than it had been used to. With a stroke of a pen, cars like the Anglia and Zephyr were rendered uncompetitive. Performance cylinder heads, carburettors and manifolds had to be junked in favour of power-strangling standard items. Ford, not one usually caught with its handbrake on, swung into action and set out to dominate saloon car racing. Walter Hayes, Ford's new Public Affairs Director, was now in control of motorsport and in 1962 he set about implementing a Cortina motorsports programme well before the car was actually launched.

Hayes was troubled by the fact that BMC were grabbing the headlines with special versions of the Mini. He came up with a cunning master plan that would involve using the rapid Cortina GT and the even swifter Lotus Cortina for the 1963 season.

The Cortina GT proved to be a very able race car

The Lotus Cortinas were homologated only late in the season but despite their belated arrival these piping hot Cortinas caused a sensation—and although only initially running with 145 bhp they were able to mix it with the much more powerful Galaxies. As the British Championship was a driver's championship, Ford could 'pick and mix' from its range of 'hot' cars. On his way to the 1963 title, Jack Sears used the ultra-reliable Cortina GT, the thundering Galaxie and—after he had won the Championship—he then got behind the wheel of a Lotus Cortina, at Oulton Park in September of that year.

The Galaxie was not such a brute when in the hands of Jack Sears.

Dan Gurney streams around a very wet Brands Hatch.

Jim Clark simply danced the Lotus Cortina around the race track.

Jack Brabham heads Jim Clark at Oulton Park 1965.

1964 was all about Jim Clark. Despite his hectic Formula One schedule he took time out to stamp his authority on the British Saloon Car Championship. Clark contested all eight rounds, won his class eight times, outright three times and took the Championship title in spectacular style. His four-wheel drifts and wheel-lifting exploits are the stuff of legend, and remain indelibly etched in many an enthusiast's mind.

Furthermore, this Championship win effectively launched the Lotus Cortina as a serious performance car.

The British Championship was not an entirely parochial affair; it attracted various American 'muscle,' cars too. Dan Gurney campaigned the first of the 'rumbling' V8s, a Chevrolet Impala and in 1965 Roy Pierpoint took another of these transatlantic interlopers, an ex-Alan Mann Racing 4.7-litre Ford Mustang, to the title.

Hidden Depths

In 1966 the game really took off, when the BRSCC announced that the Championship would be run to FIA Group 5. The new regulations were strict but commonsense—it was just the adrenalin injection this type of racing needed.

The introduction of Group 5 certainly helped raise the profile of saloon car racing in Britain, although in essence the new format was quite simple. The cars still had to retain a virtually standard outward appearance, but engine and suspension tuners were given almost unlimited freedom. They could now try to extract all they could from the power units and the newly introduced racing tyres. Enthusiasts and drivers were salivating at the mere thought.

Anglias proved that they were a force to be reckoned with.

Cars became much faster, much noisier, and more popular with spectators and drivers alike. The Group 5 racers were quite highly developed although when compared to today's high-tech touring cars they appear delightfully old fashioned.

The manufacturers welcomed Group 5, which put the emphasis on performance with a capital 'P'. If you've got it why not flaunt it? Ford, in particular, was well represented. With an inventory that included Mustangs, Falcons, Anglias and Cortinas (plus the forthcoming Escort), it had all the options covered.

Saloon car racing was on all all-time high, so much so that the already talent-filled grids were regularly 'drip-fed' with 'Formula' aces. It was not uncommon to see drivers of the calibre of Graham Hill, Jack Brabham, Jochen Rindt, Jackie Stewart, Jacky Ickx and the like, competing with semi-works drivers and a plethora of privateers. Some of the cars were also becoming stars in their own right too.

The Lotus Cortina's adolescent frailties had been overcome and the car was a legend in the making. Ford's hottest saloon car was a cracker and deserved all the accolades that were regularly being heaped upon it, but in 1966 all eyes were on its more modest sibling, the Anglia.

Group 5 certainly gave the Anglia a new lease of life and the 997 cc Broadspeed and 1293 cc Superspeed versions were the 'class of 66'—John Fitzpatrick taking the title thanks to eight class wins. The Anglia may have been bordering on the obsolete, but in its twilight years it undoubtedly made its mark on British saloon car racing. With what was a surprisingly conventional engine, the hottest Anglia still had an impressive 136 bhp at its disposal. The Anglia drivers found that they had the legs of any works Mini Cooper 'S', although 'smoking' John Rhodes did

chase Fitzpatrick hard and ended up second overall at the end of the season. 1966 was also notable for the fact that some really competitive Imps began to materialise.

Impressive!

On a good day, the dry-liner 1-litre Imp 'Rallye' engine could make eight laps without a major engine mishap—possibly! For an Imp to get to the end of a race without having purged all of its vital fluids was considered to be a minor miracle. Racing an Imp was something of a trial in the mid-1960s.

Deep pulleys, flanged liners, then Wills rings helped Fraser Imp reliability.

Pole positions—Norman Winn (left) and Alan Fraser discuss tactics with Ray Calcutt (at the wheel).
(Below) Rootes publicity shot of the Fraser Imp in the 1966 colours—white and blue with the cross of
Saint Andrew on the roof.

(Above) The Fraser Imps out in front and staying there.
(Below) Alan Fraser contemplates the future for the Fraser Imps at his Mountains Garage.

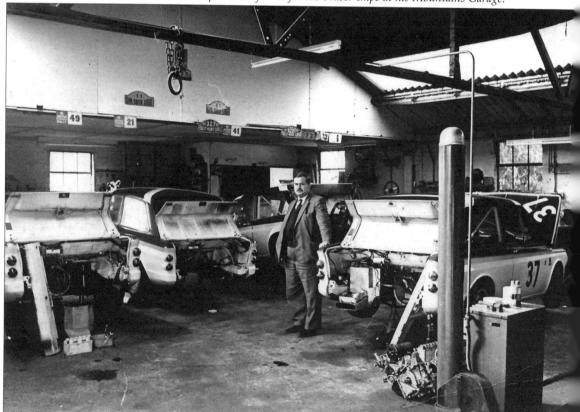

Many people became so frustrated with recurring reliability issues that they were tempted to throw Rootes's new baby out with the cooling water! By the tail end of 1966, however, the Imp had become a more dependable race car, thanks mainly to the emergence of the Fraser team.

The Imp had a tremendous number of plus points—and a tremendous number of bad ones too (not of its own making either). Rootes, keen to shift more Imps, desperately wanted the car to do an 'about turn' in terms of its reliability and, hence, image. If there was one place that the public's perception could be changed it was on the racetrack.

Impressed with what the Fraser Imps had been achieving, at the end of the 1965 season, Rootes commissioned Alan Fraser and his Mountains Garage concern to work its magic on the Imp. While Rootes tackled the production Imp's teething troubles, Fraser and his men focused on the racing versions. With meticulous attention to detail two of Fraser's key personnel, Brian Pritchard-Lovell and John Griffiths (two ex-ERA men), working with mechanic Norman Winn, resolved just about all the problems they were confronted with. The liner and gasket-sealing nightmare was overcome and as a result more power could be released.

In 1965 the Fraser Imps got some excellent results, but in 1966 they were virtually unbeatable and won their class in any championship that was open to them. Regular team drivers, Ray Calcutt, Bernard Unett and Nick Brittan between them claimed 30 wins, 19 seconds and 13 thirds. By 1967, Pritchard-Lovell and Griffiths had managed to squeeze 115 bhp from the much-modified Imp engine. Indeed, with an experimental Coventry Climax cylinder head and Lucas fuel injection, 130 bhp had been glimpsed on the dynamometer.

Unfortunately, for the Fraser team, lurking under the bonnet of it class rival, the Anglia, was another high-revving gem.

With input from Cosworth, Holbay, and when honed to perfection by Broadspeed, a Fraser-matching 115 bhp was possible from the Anglia's twin Weber carburetted 997 ccs. For 1967 approximately 124 bhp was on tap if the engine had been equipped with TJ fuel injection (with the engine canted over by 30 degrees to allow near vertical inlet tracts). Add to this package a five-speed Hewland gearbox and then it is easy to see why the Anglias were so quick. If an Imp did not win the 1-litre class then you can bet your bottom dollar it was an Anglia that did.

Change for the Better?

Initially Group 5 seemed to be working and the racing was indeed exciting, but some momentum was lost when the big manufacturers inevitably monopolised the Championship. The result being that by 1969 the racing was beginning to lose its appeal and, what is more, you could not move for Minis and Escorts.

Fitzpatrick finished second to Frank Gardner's Ford Falcon in 1967, a fitting swan song to the Anglia's career.

Bernard Unett was close behind, having hauled the Fraser Imp up to fourth place overall. The following year Gardner swapped his Falcon for a Lotus Cortina, then an Escort Twin-Cam and bagged another title.

(Above) Frank Gardner extracting the most from the big Falcon.
(Below) Frank Gardner on his way to the 1968 title in the Alan Mann Racing Lotus Cortina Mark 2.

A British Leyland Mini has already won outright the British Saloon Car Championship.* Though the race isn't over yet.

The Mini, entered by Equipe Arden and driven by Alec Poole, set the fastest lap-time in its class in seven of the ten races contested so far.

The title was clinched at Oulton Park when the Mini beat a Ford Escort to the flag in the last lap.

This means the end of American dominance in this Championship at last! And further credit to the car that's won more races and rallies than any other car in the world.

Still one race to go. But it's already all over!

Guess there's not much reason for anyone to hang around any more...

*Subject to official confirmation.

BRITISH
LEYLAND

All over- bar the shouting

What was lacking was variety. The series had quickly become the province of Ford and BMC. Nick Faure in his three-wheeling Porsche 911 was the only regular interloper. After a seven year sabbatical a Mini won the Championship.

1969 was the year of the fuel-injected Equipe Arden 970S, driven by Alec Poole.

This year was also notable in that it witnessed the emergence of a number of privately entered Imps. Of these, Mike Freeman's example was the most successful. It went well on occasions and ended twentieth in the Championship.

New Decade, New Rules

A new decade was looming, and on and off track the consensus of opinion was that the racing had become dull and predictable. In an attempt to stop the stagnation and to broaden appeal, the RAC (who had assumed control of the Championship in 1968) introduced a new class structure. For 1970, Group 2 would replace Group 5, and amongst other things the new regulations stipulated higher minimum production runs, and four useable seats.

As the new Group 2 allowed fewer modifica-

1968 was the last season for the Fraser Imps.

tions than the outgoing Group 5, everyone expected the cars to be slower. They should have known better, nothing stands still in the high octane world of motor-sport and in actual fact the racing was quicker, albeit still a little too processional.

Understandably, the changes did not meet with universal approval, and there were a few hiccups, especially in the Mini camp. Minis were going to be banned from running with 8 port heads and fuel injection. Late in the day this decision was reversed, although '5-port' development proceeded at such pace that the 8-port head was virtually superfluous. In another surprising move, Porsche's 911 was outlawed, so sadly it was time to say goodbye to this charismatic and entertaining car.

Down in what was often patronisingly referred to as the 'tiddler' class, things were looking up. The new structure would benefit the lower capacity cars—Imps in particular. With Fraser out of the picture after the 1968 season and Chrysler having withdrawn from competition at the end of 1968, Chrysler (née Rootes) was represented on the circuits by a few brave privateers. These had been 'tail-enders' in 1969 but the advent of Group 2 and the upturn in Imp race reliability meant that the door had been opened for a competitive Imp. Visitors to Chrysler's Competition Centre at Humber Road in Coventry would have certainly felt the warm glow emanating from the environs of the building. There was now the very real possibility that an Imp could win the Championship in 1970, but would it be a works-supported one? Possibly not.

In deepest Orpington a rather special Group 2 Imp was being created and the team behind this car were a very talented and a very private affair.

Porsche's 911 was squeezed out by Escorts, Minis, and rule changes.

CHAPTER 2

Family Matters

THE Bevan Imp dominated the British Saloon Car Championship for no fewer than three years, but the expertise that created it was many years in the making. George Bevan was a 'natural' with a spanner and had honed his skills to perfection by the time he had considered tackling building a racing saloon.

Mr Fix-it

The man who masterminded the team and was ultimately, if not single-handedly, responsible for its success, was George Bevan. George was born on the 17th May 1916 and from a young age was passionate about anything mechanical, especially if it happened to have wheels and an engine! Not long after he had left school George passed his driving test, got his HGV licence and began work as a long distance lorry driver. Not only were the journeys a physical challenge (the lorries were heavy, slow and unassisted), but also breakdowns were quite a common occurrence. In those pre-recovery days, drivers found themselves frequently having to fix their stricken vehicles at the roadside. George discovered that such mechanical calamities were far from being a problem to him; he actually enjoyed repairing his lorry and quickly rose to any new challenge that he met 'en route'. Do not think of him as a bush mechanic though, despite being self-taught, and without the benefit of a formal mechanical training, he was a quick learner and a meticulous worker.

It soon became obvious to all who knew him, that George was a natural mechanic and with all the practical 'hands-on' experience he was getting, he was well on the way to becoming an accomplished engineer. It was not always the lorries that required his mechanical skills either; George was an avid motorcycle enthusiast and he often had to overcome the odd 'two-wheeled' problem. His wife, Doris, remembers travelling across Salisbury Plain in George's Vincent and sidecar combination, when something sheared:

> George stopped the Vincent alongside and in view of Stonehenge. After having a good look to try and discover what had happened, he set to and made-up a replacement part from bits and pieces in his toolbox. We were soon on our way again.
>
> He actually left a spanner by the side of the road which we picked up on our return journey!

When George owned a Velocette, Doris recalls that he just could not leave it alone and was always trying to make it go faster. This did result in the occasional incident!

> We were coming through Greenwich when a valve hit the piston. George pulled over, stripped the bike down and after straightening the valve by rolling it on the edge of the pavement, he put it back in. Within no time at all we were on our way!

His reputation as a motorcycle mechanic grew, especially in club racing circles. In 1936 he began working part-time at Brands Hatch as a racing motorcycle mechanic. Doris remembers this time with great fondness:

> In those days, the races at Brands Hatch used to run the opposite way around — and there was no tarmac, just grass!

George's Vincent and sidecar

Indeed, it was not just on the trackside that his skills were valued, all the local enthusiasts used to beat a path to his door to get their lively and throbbing machines 'tweaked'. Before long, George's parents' home pulsated to the sound of Vincent, AJS, Triumph, Matchless and Norton motorbikes (George's favourite marque).

Brands Hatch 1939 style!

Front cover of the Picture Post, *July 22nd 1939. (Doris and George are both circled).*

Sensational

What was surprising was that George had been working with a disability. He had been totally deaf in one ear since the age of 11, and the hearing in his 'good' ear was far from perfect. Not that he considered his deafness to be a handicap, far from it; he simply got on with life, and trained himself to tune engines by feel. By carefully analysing the vibrations each engine gave, interpreting the sensations felt through his fingertips, he was able to glean all the mechanical information required. As the years passed by, George's deafness became more acute, but it did not seem to hinder his mechanical ability, although it did affect him in other ways, as will become clear shortly.

After marrying childhood sweetheart Doris on the 22nd June 1940, the newly-weds swapped civilian life for a spell in the army. George spent six years in the Royal Signals at Prestatyn in North Wales. Part of his job in the army involved working as a driving instructor and he spent time in Germany after the war, driving officers to official visits and functions. Doris started work as a wages clerk (little did she know, how useful this experience would prove to be in the future when charting lap times and balancing the racing budget). George left the army on the 13th April—and on the 14th he bought himself a new motorbike.

Change of Heart

Upon his return to 'Civvy Street', George briefly resumed his career as a lorry driver, but soon decided that manhandling a heavy lorry around Britain was no longer the job for him. So, he swapped the driving seat for the inspection pit and became a mechanic, albeit working for the same company. George followed this new occupation for a few years, but his natural flair with the spanner meant that he ended up doing almost all of the more difficult repairs whilst his 'colleagues' undertook the easier tasks. Aggrieved with the unfairness of his workload, George tolerated the situation for a while before he picked up his tool roll and walked!

Someone with George's skills and reputation would not be standing in the dole queue for long. Within a short space of time he had been offered employment at S. J. Meads, where he worked on forklifts used by the Port of London Authority. But, just as a career path seemed to be mapping itself out, something happened that took him in an entirely different direction.

In the 1950s, a gastronomically challenged Britain began to witness the arrival of Chinese restaurants and so began the nation's burgeoning interest in oriental food, an interest which spawned the need for specialised cooking equipment. Now as it happened George had a Chinese friend, Harry Yew. Harry had spotted an opportunity in the making; one that he thought George might be interested in. He was, and the pair got their heads together and set about designing and making a high-quality Chinese cooker for the catering trade. The fact that neither George nor Harry (who was a carpenter) had any actual experience in this field whatsoever was not perceived to be a problem. Thanks to their skilled handiwork and hard endeavour, the prototype cooker was soon completed—it looked good and, much to their delight, it worked extremely well. To enable the cooker to be sold commercially though, it had to be safety tested. Thankfully, it breezed through the rigorous tests and received the Gas Board's seal of approval. Enthused and inspired, Harry and George handed in their notices and thus was born H. & G. Gas Cooking Ranges.

Although the first cooker was a Bevan/Yew production in its entirety, the pair soon discovered a more effective option. If they bought all the individual components from specialist companies, they could assemble a cooker more quickly, and for less money.

So, it was goodbye to haulage and hello to the world of the hot crispy noodle, a world that would dominate George's everyday life, pay his bills, but not capture his heart; this part of his anatomy would forever belong to motor racing. George was an avid motor racing enthusiast and when he was not building cookers he was usually to be found at Brands Hatch, in awe of the racing.

H. & G. ENGINEERS

(Member of The Chinese Restauranteurs Association)

TELEPHONE : EAST 1807

Our Ref........................

Your Ref........................

54 TOOKE STREET,

MILLWALL,

LONDON, E.14

Harry & George's letterhead

Racing Appetite

When Peter was born it was natural that George and Doris took him to spectate at various motor racing events. Peter grew to love the racing and as soon as he was old enough, he began marshalling at events, but even this did not satiate his appetite for the sport. Returning home from one meeting, he casually announced to his father that he would like to try his hand at racing! To George, this was manna from heaven and he quickly began planning a campaign of action in readiness for the 1963 season.

Despite the racing world's growing love affair with the Mini, George and Peter decided that they wanted something a little bit different and plumped for that earliest of mass-produced 'hatchbacks', an Austin A40. It was not their first choice though. Peter had an Anglia that he was using on the road and he and George decided to prepare it for racing. However, after discussing the project with Bob Gaylor (of Baldyne Engineering then Piper Cams fame), they decided that the £350 it would have cost to prepare was way too much for the impecunious pair; they would look for a car that had already been prepared. It was not long before George had spotted a Speedwell-equipped and race-prepared 1000 cc example for sale in *Autosport*. The car had a good provenance, as it had previously belonged to racing driver, Rodney Bloore. Race-prepared the advert had stated, but on closer inspection it became apparent that it was not that special, although it did have a steel crank and rods. There was only one thing to do—they had to 'Bevan-ise' it!

Peter out in front as usual.

George was a perfectionist, and his A40 had to be the best. He and Peter set about making the little Austin sing. On its first outing at Goodwood on the 13th March 1965, Peter expertly piloted the car to a third in class beating some far more exotic machinery in the process. The engine's high power output and Peter's rapid pace meant that the car had rather an unhealthy appetite for gearboxes—it devoured one unit every two races! On only its second outing Peter equalled the Brands Hatch 1000 cc lap record (previously held by Roger Williamson, an extremely competent driver, who would go on to drive a Ferrari to 8th place in the 1967 Mexican Grand Prix. Tragically, he was killed at Zandvoort in the 1973 GP of Holland), and on its third outing he managed to take the record outright. The racing programme was successful although it was punctuated by the odd incident. During one race a wheel flew off and the car rolled out of contention. George and Peter rebuilt and then sold the A40 to racing motorcyclist, Ginger Payne, who raced under the Bevan banner for a while.

In 1966 George built Peter a 'new' A40, and he repaid his father's hard work by taking the Brands Hatch lap record from the all-conquering Fraser Imps (who it has to be said did not take too kindly to having their lap record beaten by such an 'old-tech' machine). It was at this time that George became friendly with Stuart Turner, who was persuaded to provide a short-stroke Formula 3 engine for the A40 (one that had previously been fitted to Jackie Stewart's race car). In spite of all the modifications done to the car, including the fitment of a semi-downdraught head, the opposition was getting quicker too. George somehow managed to liberate 101.8 bhp from the engine (even with the benefit of computers and other modern equipment, current race Mini 1-litre engines, admittedly without the benefit of that head and carburettor combination, are currently achieving around 95 bhp), but the Austin's bulk was proving to be a bit of a handicap. Nevertheless, Peter overcame this 'weighty' problem and was establishing himself

My, that's a big one! Peter's A40 now had an ex-Jackie Stewart short-stroke Formula 3 engine fitted.

as quite a rapid driver. On one occasion he even managed to beat a certain young chap called Jackie Oliver who was driving a much more modern and nimble Mini!

Free Spirits
It would be fair to say that the Bevan family led a nomadic existence travelling from circuit to circuit. When they were not travelling you could find them at their little place in the country—Brands Hatch!

Every Wednesday and Saturday was spent testing the race car at the Kent circuit. Back in those halcyon days there was a real family atmosphere. Indeed, decades before track days became 'de rigueur' amongst performance car fans, many enthusiasts used to bring their road cars down to have a good old thrash around the circuit. Inevitably, there were incidents and the occasional off-road 'excursion'. Friends would quickly jump to, and tow the bent and crumpled cars away from the track to some nearby lane, whence the owners would claim it was a road accident and thereby be eligible for an insurance claim!

Those days were great fun, yet such casual affairs. One unfortunate driver rolled his Mini Cooper at Paddock Bend. Not such an unusual occurrence you might think. Well this particular Mini's boot sprang open during this 'incident' and the contents of said boot were deposited all over the track. Amused spectators were treated to the sight of a lovely wicker picnic hamper, checked tablecloth, sandwiches, flask and assorted cutlery being scattered left, right and centre!

Wise words indeed.

33

British Racing and Sports Car Club
Limited

Patron: The Rt. Hon. The Earl Howe, P.C., C.B.E., V.R.D.   President: John N. Cooper.
Vice Presidents: J. Brabham, J. Clark, H. R. Godfrey, G. Hill, Maj. Gen. A. H. Loughborough, O.B.E., A. E. Moss.
General Secretary: Nicholas Syrett.

Affiliated to the R.A.C.

MALLORY PARK
SUNDAY APRIL 24th, 1966.
CLUBMAN'S CAR RACES.

INFORMATION SHEET NO.6.

EVENT NO.6.   SALOON CARS UP TO 1000c.c.   Start 5.00.
                                        (15 laps)

POSITION.	CAR NO.	ENTRANT & DRIVER.	CAR.	TIME M. S.	SPEED M.P.H.
1st	102	P. Beven	Austin A40	11.42.6	76.86
2nd	109	C.J. Toten	Austin Cooper S.	11.49.2	
3rd	112	D.H. Griffiths.	Austin Cooper.	11.50.8	
4th	114	R.J. Lee	Austin Cooper S.	11.51.8	
5th	104	R.J. Ellice	Austin Cooper S.	12.05.6	
6th	106	R.J.S. Haining.	Morris Cooper S.	12.24.2	

Fastest Lap: Car No: 102 Time: 0 mins 45.6 secs   Speed: 78.95

Non-Starters: 103,108,110,113.

Retirements: Car number 105 retired on lap 13.

Peter and the A40 were a rapid combination. This result sheet shows just how rapid!

George's deafness made him the victim of one such 'racing' incident too. Some years later, on one fateful practice day, he stepped out into the pit lane right into the path of a Formula Ford. Not hearing the car, George was caught by its wheel, which threw him into the air. He landed with a tremendous thump; so much so, he was concussed. Everyone insisted that he was taken to hospital, but George, being George, was having none of this mollycoddling and discharged himself at 6 a.m. the next day and made his own way back to Brands in time for the race!

George approached his racing with a serious and professional manner, but that is not to say that he did not have a sense of humour. One of the scrutineers at the time was Fred Matthews—a man renowned for being a bit of a stickler. Initially, George had a number of 'problems' with Fred, although he and Peter did manage to devise some rather devious ways of getting their car through scrutineering. On one occasion Fred pronounced himself unhappy with the driver's window on the A40, which did not have the mandatory aperture and declared:

> You are not racing without a hole in the window.

Rather than remonstrate with Fred, George wound the window up, then put his fist through the (fortunately brittle) Perspex proclaiming:

> Okay, here's a hole for you!

With the pounding the A40 got, the front wheel bearings were inevitably subject to some slight play and despite George's rigorous maintenance they would often cause problems at scrutineering. George, however, had an answer! When Fred went to check one side of the car, one of them would lean on the car (to shift the pressure and tighten up any slight play in the opposite wheel), and then as Fred went to check the other wheel, they would swap sides. At another event a fellow competitor and Peter were lined up awaiting scrutineering. George spotted Fred amongst the scrutineers and, to his dismay, realised that it would be Fred who would be checking their car over. George—quick thinking as ever—courteously waved a fellow competitor through, straight into Fred's hands. It has to be said that this other driver was not best pleased with the 'rigorous' scrutineering his car received! To be fair, Fred was only doing his job to the letter, and over the years they became good friends, with Fred often dropping into the Bevan household for a chat and a cup of tea.

Before we decry what would be perceived today as a rather casual approach to racing, it is worth bearing in mind that a number of racing's top names cut their teeth at these 'practice' events. Peter Bevan himself was even recording race-winning times, long before having ever entered a race.

Racing Rootes

By 1967, George felt that it was time for a change of car. The A40 was quick, but it was difficult to see how it could be made more competitive—it was time to find a new car. After thinking about an Anglia once more, George decided that the new Bevan-mobile was going to be a Hillman Imp—despite having pulled his friend and Fraser Imp racer, Ray Calcutt's leg on more than one occasion, when he had asked him why he was driving "that rubbish little car"!

It was a logical move really, because the Fraser operation was deadly serious and very well organised. Through a great deal of effort the Fraser Imps were really getting their act together and starting to shake up the established opposition grabbing the top slots from the Broadspeed Anglias and the like. It was a shame that Rootes pulled the plug on its competition participation at the end of 1968. Who knows what heights the Fraser engineers and Ian Carter (who built the engines) would have taken Imp development too? George had observed the Fraser Imp's meteoric rise up the grid with keen interest and within a short space of time, he had hatched a plan to build a racing Imp himself.

Saloon car fans out in force!

The Bevan club-racing Imp was built (using an early second-hand car as its basis) during 1967. From the outset, it utilised 998 cc and 850 cc engines depending upon the event.

Interestingly, George achieved the 850 cc capacity in a variety of ways. One was to use the 875 bore and have the crankshaft ground to suit, but for the real screamers he opted for the 998 cc (72.5 mm) pistons and liners and had the crankshaft ground to give a miniscule 51.25 mm stroke. No wonder that these ultra short-stroke engines used to rev to over 11,000 rpm!

George always thought that the 850 engine was very good and not the limp-wristed poor relation that its reduced capacity might suggest. He did such an engine for Mini ace-to-be Rob Mason and Rob shook up the opposition by posting a stunning practice lap at Brands Hatch, some 3 seconds below the lap record.

He even managed to record a similar time during the race. Of course, there were a few long faces and much muttering, so it came as no surprise to George when the scrutineers decided to have the engine stripped. George pulled the head off, and after the bore and stroke were checked, it was discovered that the engine was not in fact an 850, it was an 840—some 10 cc below the class limit!

George built similar capacity engines for a few other racers, and one of his Finnish ice racing customers, Juhani Kynsilehto would suffer the same problem over in Finland. After decimating the opposition with his Bevan 850, a protest was registered, and his car was stripped and found to be 840 cc too. Sensing the humour of the situation, Kynsilehto promptly sent a tongue-in-cheek telegram to George asking him where were the other 10 ccs he had paid for and please could he have a refund!

In addition to Minis, Rob Mason would race Bevan Imps with great success. (Imp pictured is 1975 Kent Messenger Championship *winning car).*

Free Thinker

George was a pioneer, and he used the club-racing Imp as a test bed to try out a number of his less orthodox tuning ideas. One novel feature of the early Imp was a very special front suspension arrangement. Ever since the Imp's inception, the tuners had for some time been experimenting with ways to improve upon the Imp's drum brakes and swing-axle suspension (the swing-axle suspension had been fitted to all production Imps for entirely practical reasons and, given its design limitations, the set-up worked very well). George approached the problem from an entirely different angle—literally! His Imp utilised Triumph Herald front uprights and discs, which were grafted on so professionally that they looked like a standard factory fitment. The set-up had been designed and installed by Tony Hilder of Piper fame. Despite looking the business, having disc brakes, and endowing the Imp with a turning circle that would not have disgraced a London Taxi, it did not perform quite as well as the original Imp swing-axle suspension. It was lighter, though.

Not content with altering the front suspension, George also exercised a degree or two of inventiveness (drawing upon his motorcycle experience) with the carburation and the exhaust system. He decided to graft copper pipes on to the trumpets of the Imp's Weber carburettors, and this cut-price injection system fed a fine spray of petrol into each of the trumpets. The exhaust manifold came in for some treatment too. George fashioned it into four separate pipes, each of which had its own motorcycle type megaphone exhaust. It looked and sounded brilliant, but George soon decided that a motorcycle approach to tuning may well have suited the Vanwall Formula One car, but it did not do the Imp any favours. The power output was not quite as good as had been hoped. Before long, the injection system and the French horn-type pipework had been ditched in favour of normal Weber carburation and Janspeed exhaust system.

Rare picture of the first ever race with the club Imp (right), at the first ever race at Thruxton in 1968 after its redevelopment. Peter made a stunning start and went on to win the race.

Table Top Racer

As with all of George's cars, the Imp was immaculately turned out and prepared to the highest standards. The family had moved to 62 Leesons Hill and as nice a house as it was, it did not actually have a garage. This seems barely credible today, when one thinks of the facilities that racing teams usually have at their disposal. When anything serious had to be done to the car, he used his next-door neighbour's garage and this was none too spacious either. All the early engine building had to be done on the very tolerant Mrs Bevan's kitchen table—and visitors to the house would often have to eat their meals with an Imp race engine for company!

It was not as if Doris got any help around the house in way of compensation. George was not fond of housework; indeed, he did not do anything in the house,

Even with Triumph front suspension the Imp still picked a front wheel up when driven hard

Leader of the pack

domestic or D.I.Y. It was not that he could not do things, he just would not. Doris used to do everything as far as the housework and family were concerned and if something needed doing to the house, then George would pay someone else to do it. As for the lawn and garden? As far as George was concerned, these were places that he had to negotiate on the way to his shed-cum-workshop!

The kitchen was a veritable mechanical storehouse too. Doris Bevan kept things extremely neat and tidy, but open any cupboard and you were likely to discover camshaft bearings nestling alongside packets of cereals and the like. Even the family freezer was occasionally pressed into action as a makeshift storage container and was a good tool for freezing valve guides prior to their insertion in the cylinder head. George did make the occasional concession mind you; he took the bits and pieces out of the kitchen over the Christmas period, well Christmas Eve and Christmas Day that is. Come Boxing Day it was back to normal, with valves nestling up to vinegar bottles, pistons alongside potatoes, camshaft bearings by cereal boxes, 'et al'!

Life in the Bevan kitchen was like the interpretation on this Newton birthday card - it must have been because Doris sent this card to George!

Peter raced the Imp initially, and remembers revelling in the delights of rack and pinion steering but, inevitably, marriage intervened and by May he had vacated the driving seat, although he was still involved in the preparation and construction of the car. Peter was skilled behind the wheel, but he was also very capable at extracting the most power possible from cylinder heads and in the mid-sixties he had worked for Baldynes, then Pipers, then for himself, in preparing cylinder heads. In fact, Peter did the cylinder head for a race Mini that belonged to James Hunt and although not credited for it, he also designed and

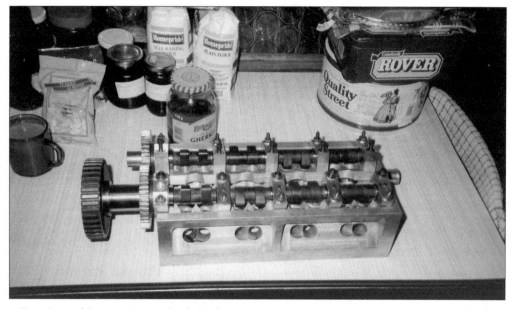

Experimental Bevan twin-cam head vies for space on the kitchen table with Doris Bevan's Christmas cake ingredients—you'd have to be careful when biting into the Christmas pudding too— you could have found more than the odd threepenny bit!

developed the famous 'angle' head for the Imp, otherwise known in Imp circles, as the Chesman 'wedge' head. This radical design involved machining huge amounts off the cylinder head and some rewelding and refacing. The process was very labour intensive, but it allowed the head, manifold and carburettors to be at a much better angle, which released more power. Another Imp guru, Andy Chesman, did the machining for these heads at his Coventry-based Greetham Engineering concern; hence the fact that the wedge head is normally attributed to him. Of course (and rather sadly, bearing in mind the 'special' heads that other manufacturers managed to homologate), this head was not eligible for the British Championship.

George had been well and truly bitten by the Imp bug, and in his 'spare' time, had designed and built an Imp-powered motorcycle and sidecar outfit. When the sidecar world adopted the Imp engine, outfits powered by Bevan engines regularly beat the factory Hondas, until the time Honda introduced their very powerful two-strokes.

Peter was finding the cylinder head work to be a bit of a grind, so in 1968 he left the world of gas 'flowing' behind (as far as his daily employment was concerned) and entered the world of gas 'cooking'—he joined the family business, took over the brunt of the workload and immersed himself in its day-to-day activities.

It was not long after he had made this career change that the cooker business began to slow down. There was not quite enough work to sustain both Peter and George, so Peter encouraged his father to start a tuning business and he would run the family business single-handedly. But, just when it seemed that the new tuning

Peter really getting to grips with the club Imp, ahead of Jon Mowatt's Mini.

Brian Howton and Tony Dingle at speed on their Bevan-powered sidecar outfit.

venture was about to take off, the demand for Chinese food, and hence cookers, soared. So, it was back to 'wok' for George!

It is important to emphasise that all Bevan Imps, engines etc, were initially built as a hobby, and contrary to popular opinion, George Bevan never ever ran a tuning business 'per se', although George and his mechanics did build numerous engines and a few cars for favoured friends and customers. It would also be fair to say that what started as a recreation soon became a way of life to George.

All Change

With Peter out of the driving seat, George began shopping around for a new driver and as it happened, saloon car 'hot-shot' Bill McGovern was on the market. With Paul Emery having pulled out of racing, Bill was without a drive. He had 'told' *Autosport* that he was retiring in the hope that someone would spot this news and offer him a drive. Fortunately, George was an avid *Autosport* reader and saw the piece. He was quick to act and snapped Bill up. George had respected Bill's ability for some time and he suspected that the combination of Bill plus a fast, reliable Imp would be a winning one—and it did not take long for his suspicions to be confirmed. The Bevan/McGovern partnership worked from the off and over the next few years the two would become saloon car racing's finest 'double act'. Acquiring the services of Bill McGovern was a very shrewd move and was undoubtedly a major factor in the success of the Bevan Imp.

Bill McGovern pushing hard in a Paul Emery Imp.

Peter had not completely left the scene though, as he still prepared the heads for all of his father's cars and for a number of other people. Whilst George was away racing, Peter was left at the helm and often remembers seeing the Imp on its trailer going one way up the motorway, while he was heading in the opposite direction in a van loaded down with cookers and spare parts. Such is life!

Bill's first race in the Bevan club-racing Imp was at Brands Hatch and he quickly got into the groove revelling in the performance, handling and above all, the reliability of his new steed. He drove well—very well, and went on to win the BBC 'TV Trophy' series that year, which was centred on Lydden. This and the excellent coverage the series received ensured that the Bevan equipe began to be noticed. The following year the team continued to notch up wins, although not everything went so smoothly. At Crystal Palace, Bill had to lift off to avoid a slower Mini, and as he swerved a shock absorber tore free from its mounting and within moments Bill's world turned upside down as the Imp inverted itself. Thankfully, Bill walked away from what was quite a major accident unscathed but the same could not be said of the Imp—it was a complete write-off.

George and Bill often cast a discerning eye in the direction of the British Saloon Car Championship (George checked some of the lap times and was surprised to discover that the club Imp had been circulating faster than the Group Five cars!). Bill and Peter felt that George should perhaps set his sights a little higher than club events and eventually he was cajoled into building a car with which they could tackle not only club events, but the RAC Saloon Car Championship as well.

A slightly apprehensive-looking Bill McGovern in the Bevan Imp just before the off.

CHAPTER 3

Pocket Rocket

A NEW bodyshell would have been nice, but George rarely bought new cars, even to convert to racers. The decision was made, therefore, to base the Group 2 car on a second-hand Imp. This was not just a pocket-saving move, it was practical one too—a complete car would provide all those fiddly and difficult to obtain bits and pieces, which would have taken an age to source from dealers and suppliers.

In less than a month after its predecessor had bitten the dust, George had the new Imp up and running. This car would form the basis of the Group 2 challenger although it would be used in club events until the start of the 1970 season (in 850 cc, 998 cc and 1092 cc forms).

Bodybuilding

George scoured the classifieds and within no time at all he had found an unmarked low-mileage Imp, which he acquired for the princely sum of £315. Contemporary reports always cited this car as being a 1969 Sunbeam Imp Sport. Not so. Research shows it was, in fact, a Bermuda Blue 1966 'E' registration Hillman Imp Mark 2 Deluxe, chassis number B4120191254150.

George Bevan fabricated alloy fuel tank (note the mandatory 'splash' guard).
The tank also utilised the existing mounting points to stop bodyshell flexing.

Purchasing this 'early' Imp was a sound move because mid-sixties Imps were undoubtedly better put-together than later examples. Many enthusiasts even support the notion that the metal used on Imps during this period is of a higher quality (although there is no hard evidence to support this). What is certain is that there are many more spot welds on the early cars, which is a definite plus point when it comes to structural rigidity. What-ever their particular Imp predilection, the cognoscenti generally point to 1966 as being a 'vintage' year in terms of construction and quality.

Bill McGovern's 'office'.

Suspension Low-down

With a number of club events still on the calendar and the 1970 season rapidly approaching, George knuckled down and set about effecting the Imp's transformation from shopping car to race star and he began by tackling the all-important suspension.

From late 1967 onwards, Imps were equipped with low-pivot front suspension, which reduced understeer and sharpened up their on-road handling considerably. Due to its date of manufacture, the donor Imp obviously predated this factory-introduced modification and was blessed with the original and somewhat 'knock-kneed' high-pivot suspension—not the best option for a potential race Imp! Of course, this had to go and George converted the car to the later low-pivot specification

Low-pivot suspension is fine for the road, but to get an Imp to really handle on the track, two important modifications have to be undertaken. Firstly the ride height needs to be set as low as possible. Secondly, for the wide, stiff and low-profile racing tyres to work properly, the camber changes inherent with the Imp's front swing-axle and rear semi-trailing suspension have to be limited.

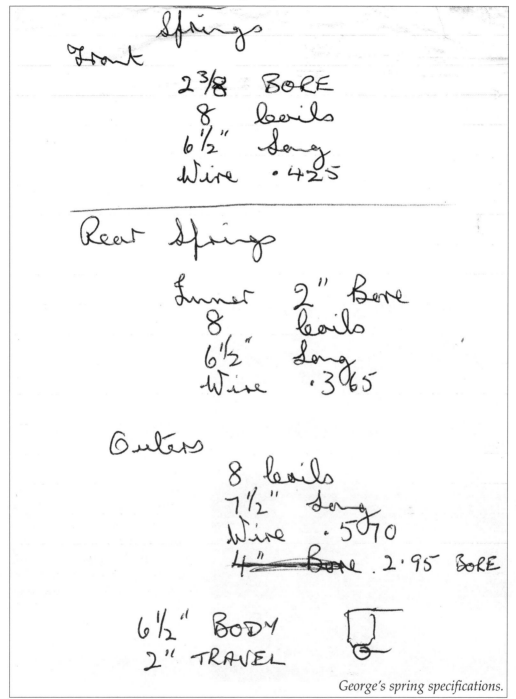

Front Springs

    2 3/8 BORE
    8 coils
    6 1/2" long
    Wire .425

Rear Springs

    Inner 2" Bore
    8 coils
    6 1/2" long
    Wire .365

Outers

    8 coils
    7 1/2" long
    Wire .570
    4" Bore .2.95 BORE

6 1/2" BODY
2" TRAVEL

George's spring specifications.

Up front, the longish standard 195 lb springs were replaced by ultra short ones (rated at 350 lb) and these were controlled by race specification Armstrong adjustable shock absorbers. George then machined and shimmed sets of stub axles, so that the camber could be 'fine tuned' to suit wet or dry conditions. An anti-roll bar was also added. This was fashioned from 11/16 -inch diameter tubing and rose-jointed at its outer ends. The original suspension arms were retained, but these were seam-welded and boxed-in at the innermost ends.

At the rear of the car, the story was much the same. To cope with the enormous cornering loads the car would regularly endure, stronger (Imp Van) semi-trailing arms were used. These were seam welded and strengthened both internally and a 'strap' was welded around the bearing housing.

To enable the car to sit as low as the driveshaft angle would allow, the original 475 lb springs were binned and in their place went extremely short and very stiff (up to 750 lb rate) race springs. These were 'assisted' by 100 lb inners (a George Bevan innovation) that sat on a 'top hat,' which nestled in the bottom of the spring seat. Often the springs were supplemented by Aeon rubber bump stops. The idea behind the double spring and bump stop system was to give the Imp some small degree of suspension progression, which would help settle the car into the corners. Keeping the Imp's rear weight bias under control were expensive Koni race shock absorbers, adjustable for bump and rebound.

Lowering the rear introduced the inevitable negative camber. To counter this

problem and provide scope for adjustment, George purchased a couple of new rear suspension crossmembers — which he then machined, strengthened and shimmed to vary the pivot points. These, like the modified front stub axles, allowed some camber adjustment and were changed to suit weather conditions or track require-ments.

Although it utilised a number of race-quality (and expensive) substitutions, the Bevan Imp's front suspension was still remarkably similar to its production counterpart.

Rose-jointed anti-roll bar (note that the bodywork has been 'notched' to provide the clearance for the bar).

Wheel-right

The Imp rolled along on Minilite magnesium alloy wheels (although during some of the 1972 events, the car did occasionally appear on Revolution alloys), which were almost always George's wheel of choice. The Bevan Imp used a variety of widths and different offsets depending on circumstances. The magnesium Minilite scored on a number of counts: due to its inherent strength there was no danger of failure and magnesium construction makes for extreme lightness that reduces the unsprung weight and improves handling. The classic 8-spoke design also allows for efficient brake cooling—useful when trying to slow an Imp from 136 mph! Then, of course, there is the matter of aesthetics—they look good, too.

Minilite wheels under the beautiful hand-formed wheel arches.

Engin-eering

If you had lifted the Bevan Imp's fibreglass engine lid you would have seen a extremely tidy and relatively normal looking engine bay. Of course, appearances can be deceptive. The heart of the Bevan engine was a standard Chrysler Competition Department wet-liner 998 cc block with final machining and checking being done by Jacey Plastics in Erith, Kent. All the reciprocating parts were checked and crack-tested by Thompson Engineering, SE19.

George shunned the traditional works R23 full-race camshaft, preferring instead to begin his campaign with a Piper IRPGB (GB standing for George Bevan). This profile had been specially developed for the Bevan Imp. Together with a Peter Bevan head, a pair of Weber DCOE (or occasionally Dellorto) carburettors and a large bore Fraser inlet/exhaust manifold it helped the engine deliver a lusty 110 bhp, nearly three times the power of a standard Imp!

(Above) Immaculate engine bay: a George Bevan trademark.

(Below) Amazing Fraser-type race exhaust manifold (note the extreme driveshaft angles).

Ration-ing

The regulations dictated that the standard casing had to be retained, but the internals could be replaced by something altogether more suitable and these came in the form of Jack Knight straight-cut and dog-engagement gears. Not only were these much stronger, they were available in a huge choice of ratios. This enabled the Imp's gearing to be tailored to suit the requirements of the different circuits or engine modifications.

By virtue of its rear-engine configuration the Imp was blessed with inherently good traction, but, to get as much power onto the track as possible, a Jack Knight limited slip differential was also installed. George being George, did not just fit and forget, he also adjusted the suspension settings to counteract the 'slipper's' natural tendency to promote understeer.

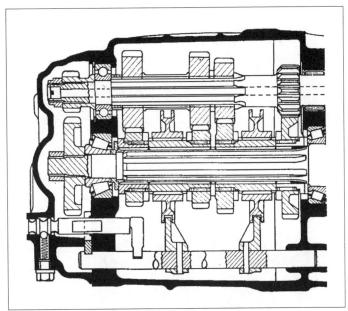

Jack Knight transaxle arrangement.

Underfloor Heating

Standard Imps have a neatly packaged rear-mounted radiator, which is somewhat marginal in terms of its ability to cool even the standard 39 bhp engine. Competition Imps, almost universally, have the water radiator repositioned at the nose of the car, which necessitates long pipe runs through the cabin of the car. George, ever tidy, thought up his own way of plumbing in the waterworks. He was not going to have pipes running through his car, they looked ugly and overheated the driver—his Imp's interior was not going to become a mobile sauna!

Pipework was bread and butter to George and he fabricated the pipes in such a way that they were able to run underneath the car and clear the front suspension, even when on full droop. Very neat and very clever.

The all-important radiator was a rather special affair, based on a F3 design and incorporated an oil cooler (in many ways, it was very similar to the unit pioneered on the Fiat Abarth 850 & 1000 race cars circa 1964). Air was able to pass through each matrix unhindered, and then vented through small drillings in the front luggage compartment and a large cutout in the spare wheel well.

Radiator piping (note anti-roll bar and notched wishbones)

An oil cooler mounted in the engine compartment, or better still ahead of a front-mounted radiator would have done the job relatively effectively, but this arrangement tends to preheat the airflow through the water radiator. Competition Imp engines are much more reliable, if oil and water temperature remain constant for the duration of an event. The very long pipe runs that the front-mounted oil cooler dictated were not a problem to George. He just routed them through the sills, where the heater hoses once resided—brilliant!

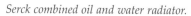

Serck combined oil and water radiator.

Spare wheel-well cut out, (note SU electric fuel pump, oil cooler piping and wishbone strengthening).

On occasions, the bonnet was packed up slightly at the rear to help expel even more hot air.

Brake-down

For the first few events of the 1970 season, Imps had to run with the standard drum brakes. The most that could be done to uprate them was to fit Ferodo fade-resistant VG95 linings and bolt on a servo, which was exactly what George did. When front discs were homologated, the improvement in braking was enormous. The Vauxhall Viva discs, Girling alloy callipers and Ferodo DS11 pads worked in absolute harmony with the rear drums. Indeed, when sufficient pressure was applied to the brake pedal, the Bevan Imp seemingly welded itself to the tarmac! Braking stability was also greatly improved. But, there was a trade-off.

Fitting these discs had the effect of increasing the track by 3/4-inch each side. As a result, the tyre/wheelarch clearance (already marginal) was further compromised. Also, the wider track had the effect of softening the spring rate, which meant that the ride height dropped slightly, and the camber became a touch more negative. All of which, of course, George took into consideration when sorting out the suspension settings.

Girling alloy calliper and Viva disc.

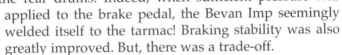

Crunch Time

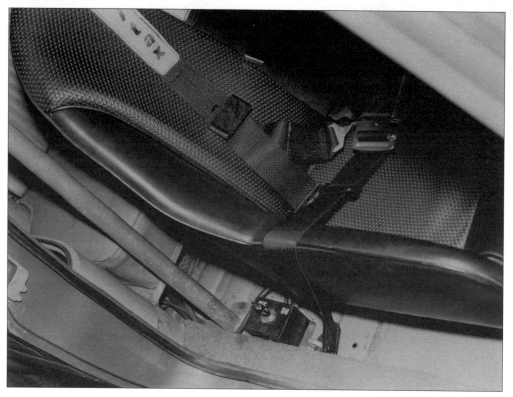

Britax harness, Corbeau seat, roll-over hoop and cut-out switch.

As with most cars competing at the time, driver protection was, at best, rudimentary. Nonetheless, the Bevan Imp was equipped with the best items available at the time.

The roll cage on the club-racing Imp had been constructed from gas tubing (what else would George have used!), but the British Championship car utilised a pukka John Aley device. This comprised of a single hoop with small stays that located on the inner wheelarches. No front cage was fitted during the first or second season. As regulations changed and technology improved, the car would eventually sport a much beefier rear cage complete with diagonal. A strong and well-secured Corbeau bucket seat and a Britax racing harness held Bill's buttocks and torso firmly in place.

Build Totals

The pace of the Bevan Imp is all the more impressive when the weight of the car is taken into consideration. At 14.25 cwt, it was way above the class minimum and could really have done with a bit of a diet. Talking of pounds, the total build cost, including the purchase of the base vehicle, was estimated as being between £1,500 to £2,000. Not over the top expensive, but not bargain-basement either.

All Change!

The single defining factor in the Bevan Imp's success was preparation. Nothing, however small, was ever left to chance. The car was built to an incredibly high standard and George's maintenance schedule was rigorous to say the least—and expensive!

Regardless of the use it was put too, each engine was completely rebuilt after every three races. Pistons and rods were renewed after every four races.
After each race the following were changed:
- Main and big-end bearings.
- Driveshaft couplings (and after *every* practice).
- Tyres.
- Oil and filter.

Brake pads, shoes, discs, drums, were changed according to wear rate, as this was circuit dependent.

What did *not* change was the car. The same car was used to win the Championship in 1970, 1971 & 1972. It was never reshelled, just refreshed!

Car specification at the beginning of the 1970 season

BODYSHELL
Second-hand 1966 Mark 2 Hillman Imp De Luxe.
Aley Bars roll-over hoop.
Corbeau seat.
Britax harness.
Weight 14.25 cwt.

COLOUR
Electric Blue.

ENGINE
998 cc all-alloy in line four-cylinder wet-liner.
Imp Sport cylinder head.
1.4-inch inlets / 1.125-inch exhausts.
11.25:1 compression ratio.
Piper IRPGB camshaft.
Competition cam carrier, drilled to provide oil flow to all 8 cam followers.
Twin Weber DCOE 40 carburettors (with rampipes but no air filter).
Combined inlet and exhaust manifold.
Standard Chrysler Competition tuftrided crankshaft.
Standard rods, lightened, shotpeened, balanced & matched.
Vandervell competition bearings.
Champion R60 spark plugs.
Castrol R40 oil.
Adjustable oil pressure relief valve (65 lbs/sq. in pressure when hot).
Maximum Power 110 BHP @ 8800 rpm.
Torque 72 lb/ft @ 7600 rpm.

COOLING SYSTEM
Serck combined oil and water radiator (front mounted).

PETROL
SU electric pump, 9 gallon or 15.25-gallon alloy tanks to suit, depending on the event.

TRANSMISSION
Four-speed manual, Jack Knight straight cut gears with LSD, gears changed for specific circuits.

BRAKES
Front: 8-inch drums.
Rear: Standard drums with VG 95 linings.
Servo assistance.

SUSPENSION – FRONT
Swing-arm, 350 lb coil springs, anti-roll bar and telescopic Armstrong dampers.

SUSPENSION – REAR
Semi-trailing Imp Van arms, 750 lb outer coil springs, 100 lb inner helpers, Aeon rubber bump stops and telescopic double-acting race Koni dampers.

WHEELS
Minilite magnesium, 6-inch or 7-inch (front), 8-inch or 9-inch (rear) depending on track conditions.

TYRES
Dunlop 4.75/10 (front), 4.75/11 (rear).

PERFORMANCE
0-60: 7seconds.
Top Speed: 136 mph.

CHAPTER 4

1970 and all that

B EFORE the 1970 season George had become one of Baldyne Engineering's more regular clients and he spent many an hour there setting up the Imp engines. Because of his deafness, George sat in the test bay without earplugs whilst the engines were put through their paces! Many sessions later and satisfied with the static testing, George gathered everything and everyone together and set off in the direction of Brands Hatch for some 'active' testing. There was a new face in the group too, as George had secured the services of mechanic, Keith Tilbrook. The Group 2 Bevan Imp certainly looked full of intent, but could it cut it on the track with the RAC crowd?

Testing Times

When they arrived at Brands they discovered that the 1969 Champion, Alec Poole, was also there with his Mini (was this simply fate?—or prior knowledge!).

Alec Poole in the Arden 970S.

Bill McGovern wheeled the immaculate Bevan Imp out on to the track and much to everyone's surprise (George included) Bill began circulating at over a second a lap quicker than the Mini. Poole with the 115 bhp Mini was in the 60-second bracket with McGovern comfortably achieving a 59.1.

Bill recalls:

> Brands is my favourite circuit and I was always quick there. Alec Poole had the Arden Mini out testing and demonstrating it to some assembled journalists. There were a few surprised and one or two long faces after the Imp's lap times were posted!

Bill giving the 'Hillman' Imp some serious welly!

Suitably encouraged, George then entered the Imp in eight club events in quick succession. Eight class wins later George felt that he had the right tool for the job, and the future looked rosy. In one race Bill had beaten John Turner's rapid and multi-Championship-winning Imp. Having done so, George could now justifiably lay claim to the fact that the Bevan Imp was, in all likelihood, the fastest Imp in the world.

Here we go... here we go... here we go!

After much input from all concerned, the big day finally arrived. The Bevan equipe was about to make the quantum leap from club racing to saloon car racing at the highest national level. The team arrived at Brands Hatch circuit with one immaculate Imp, a comprehensive package of spares and three engines (one practice engine, a fresh one for the race, and a spare).

Unless there were circumstances beyond his control, George's strategy never changed. After completing the first practice session, the team would replace the practice engine with the race engine. Bill would run this in during the second practice session, (putting in three fast final laps to help bed it in). If the race engine had performed to expectations, then it was retained for the race, otherwise the spare was slotted in.

Contrary to what the doubting Thomases and other people (usually less successful competitors and frustrated team managers) often implied; there never was a 'special' or larger capacity practice engine. All the engines were built to an identical specification. There was only ever one modification made to the car for the practice sessions—to lower it as far as was possible.

Lowering the Imp helped reduce the lap times, but there was a trade-off: the resultant extreme driveshaft angles also reduced the rubber Rotoflex couplings to quivering wrecks. George devised a special ball and socket joint to secure the driveshaft, should the overworked couplings ever give up their unequal struggle. This modification was not used during the actual races because George felt it would have contravened the ruling that no extra metal be added to the structure of the car—after all, George was Mr Legality!

McGovern fired up his Group 2 'pocket rocket,' snaked and screeched his way down the pit lane before roaring out on to the track in his typically exuberant manner. This macho 'display' was done purely and simply to gain a psychological advantage over his competitors. In fact, despite these pit lane antics, Bill almost always ran a very slow first lap, usually some 10, if not even 20 seconds off his typical pace. Having completed this first 'shakedown' lap, he would absolutely floor the throttle and leave all the other contenders in his wake: cautious, or smart?

Race 1   Brands Hatch   22 March 1970

It was not going to be an easy début for the Bevan Imp, despite the race being held at Bill McGovern's favourite track, Brands Hatch. Due to certain parts not yet having been homologated, Imps had to use a number of standard components —components that were hard pressed to cope, even with the production Imp's 39 bhp! The main foci of concern were the clutch and the driveshaft couplings and there was much crossing of fingers and stroking of rabbit's feet going on amongst the Bevan team.

In practice, the concerns proved to well founded, although the first mechanical failure was an unforeseen one. During lap 10, the Bevan Imp broke a rear suspension link, which in turn inflicted fatal damage on the Rotoflex driveshaft coupling. This offending item was changed, as was its partner and George made a note to reinforce the links prior to the next race (they had already been uprated—but obviously not enough).

Frank Gardner and his Camaro were on pole for this two-part race, but the rest of the field consisted almost entirely of Escorts and Minis. Despite Ford's best intentions, only one 1300 cc Escort (but with almost 150 bhp at its disposal), had made it to the grid, piloted by John Fitzpatrick. As if to rub salt into the wound, there were no less than ten 1300 cc Minis to keep it company! In the first race, Bill McGovern should have been competing against rapid Scots racer, Gerry Birrell (who had previously raced the 1180 cc Coventry-Climax-engined Perdal-Chamois and would tragically be killed in a Formula 2 race at Rouen in 1973).

Unhappy at having to run on drum brakes Birrell withdrew from the race. This left only two other Imps in the up-to-1-litre class, those belonging to Mike Freeman and Jim Howden. As the 970 S was no longer eligible, Mini men Viv Church and Jeremy Bean had to rely on using a brace of 998 Mini Coopers. Sparring with Bill McGovern was Vince Woodman who began his championship campaign with a Broadspeed-built fuel-injected BE1-engined, twin-cam 1-litre Escort. This beast could even out-rev most of the Imps, running easily to 9,800 rpm and having the potential to reach a dizzy 10,250 rpm. It was reputed to produce 72 ft/lbs of torque and 128 bhp, but perhaps these horses were not quite as muscular nor had as good a pedigree as the Imp's!

Out in front from the start—but not for too long.

Ford had done its homework and knew that an Imp could walk away with the Championship by virtue of consistent class wins. Vince was Ford's 'cat amongst the pigeons', placed there as a 'blocking car' to try and prevent an Imp getting to the front. Vince would be trying to sweep away the Imps and Minis and get his 1-litre screamer to the podium on as many occasions as possible. The larger-engined and gruff sounding Escorts were also expected to win their class and steadily accrue enough points to get Ford the Championship win they coveted.

Unfortunately, Ford had not counted on the speed and soon-to-be-found reliability of the Bevan Imp. The 1600 cc Escorts were extremely rapid and the 1300 cc examples were no slouches either. But, as quick as they were, they still had to navigate their way through a veritable horde of Minis, a number of which showed enormous speed from their venerable but potent 'A' series engines.

In spite of the potential that the Bevan Imp had displayed in practice—plus the fact that McGovern had comfortably led his class in the first heat—the Imp was forced to pit on lap 7 when another Rotoflex coupling had cried enough.

In heat 2, the Imp had only just moved away from the start line when the standard clutch, struggling with a surfeit of horsepower, let go. The resulting colossal over-revving caused the engine to ventilate itself and one piston (which obviously had not read the script regarding replacement intervals) made a premature bid for freedom (there is only so much over-revving that even a George Bevan engine can stand!). As consolation, the Imp had recorded the fastest lap in the first heat. Freeman won the class, with Bean in second place and Howden in third.

Race 2   Snetterton   27 March 1970

The Good Friday Guards International Meeting was an altogether more successful outing. In an attempt to discover the reasons behind the suspension failure, George had gone over the car with the proverbial fine toothcomb. Anything which looked less than one hundred per cent was replaced, and in an effort to aid reliability, new couplings, bolts, and even a new rear suspension crossmember were fitted.

George had rummaged through his stock of engines and elected to fit engine number one and head number one, although he retarded the ignition timing by five degrees because it seemed happier with that setting. The gearing was also attended to and the ratios were 13.0, 8.8, 6.5 and 5.3.

He had also searched through his 'clutch' of clutches and came across one example that had a firmer diaphragm pressure than the others. In fact, this is all that the Chrysler Competitions Department ever used to do. Their much-vaunted competition clutch covers were, in reality, no more than hand-picked standard items, and sold at a substantial price premium. A competition Imp clutch cover could be up to twenty per cent stronger, but it could also have been no better than a standard clutch cover!

A few more stickers, a little more reliability.
(Below) Amazing sight of Vince Woodman thrashing the Escort 1-litre to within an inch of its life
as he chases the Bevan Imp!

Race 3   Thruxton   30 March 1970

As the engine and transaxle had run so well at Snetterton, George elected to check them over and retain them for this race. Thruxton was apparently the cue for all the other Imps to run into trouble, while the Bevan-mobile ran faultlessly for each of its 46 laps.

Despite having to be cautious due to worries about clutch and coupling longevity, Bill had a tremendous race. He bagged another fastest lap, the lap record, 17th overall, and the class win ahead of Woodman—whose Escort unfortunately suffered from a persistent misfire and then to add insult to injury, a puncture. This car was potentially faster than the Bevan Imp, but Woodman would eventually despair of its unreliability and subsequently he would move up to the 1300 class—not handing the class to the Bevan Imp as such, but helping it nonetheless. It was a shame that the 1-litre Escort was so unreliable because it could have given the Bevan Imp some terrific competition in its class and would have been a serious contender for the Championship.

Race 4   Silverstone   26 April 1970

Silverstone saw the Bevan Imp's run of success continue. McGovern had got the measure of the standard componentry, and drove around their inherent problems—quickly!

Bill McGovern drifted the Imp through the field during the wet practice and kicked spray in his competitors' faces as they struggled to post a good lap time. In the cold but dry race he achieved another fastest lap, a class win and 13th overall. Not only did the Bevan Imp finish higher up the order than was expected, but to get an idea of how quick it was, it finished right on the tail of Richard Longman's torquey and very rapid 1300 cc Cooper S. This, understandably, was equipped with all the bells and whistles a Mini man could possibly hope for. Things seemed to bode well for the Imp.

Clubbing   3 May 1970

Although there was a lot of pressure on the team, the Bevan Imp put in an appearance at Brands Hatch club meeting and walked away with a 1st overall. It was all part of a learning curve for George as at a practice session ten days later, the springs were changed for slightly lower rated ones, which, according to George's notes, improved handling.

Dressed to Kill

Crystal Palace was the next venue and the Bevan Imp looked the business. As with all the other Imps in the Championship, the Bevan Imp had started the season as a Hillman, only to become a Sunbeam by the time it arrived at Crystal Palace. This 'badge-engineering' was done in order to qualify for all the goodies, which by now had been homologated for Chrysler's sporting Imp derivative, the Sunbeam Sport.

Flaunting its newly homologated parts: the Bevan Imp positively bristled with confidence. New in the bodywork department were Perspex side and rear windows, fibreglass bonnet and boot. A sintered F3 clutch assembly ensured that the power got on to the track—and that the conrods stayed inside the engine block! Competition 'Metalastik' driveshaft 'doughnuts' with their steel inserts, proved to be a much tougher proposition than the standard couplings. But, what really made this Imp stand out from the crowd was the famous 'eyebrow' wheelarches.

Standard arches placed severe limitations on the width of the tyre that could be squeezed within their confines. George poured over the rulebook and came up with a solution. He had his friend and 'body' man, Peter Ramford, flare the Imp's metalwork to enable the fitment of road-roller size tyres. These 1970s 'flares' looked simply great and their appearance stunned the class opposition.

Chrysler's Competition Department was impressed with Peter Ramford's results too; they quickly despatched a man to Leesons Hill to measure his handiwork and take moulds. From these moulds were soon to emerge some of the loveliest set of spats (apart from those magnificent items fitted to the Mk 1 Escorts) ever to adorn a car. Not only were they practical, but they would also give the Imps a definite psychological advantage.

Dressed to kill, driven to thrill!

Soon all the other Imps underwent a similar metamorphosis and sprouted the 'works' arches, as they had become known. Strange as it may seem, George elected to retain the hand beaten steel originals for quite some time, getting his money's worth out of them (and while he could still manage to squeeze in ever-widening racing tyres).

Here I come!

Race 5   Crystal Palace   25 May 1970

No crash dramas as in 1968 thankfully, and the Imp ran like a train—an express train! It was not slow before, but with lots of homologated Group 2 appendages fitted, the steroidal Imp flew along in practice and was easily quickest in its class. Despite this successful practice session, George decided that the Imp could be made to go even quicker, so in the lunch break he and Keith Tilbrook changed the springs, and on the race engine they fitted a hotter camshaft and a new design of exhaust manifold. Phew!

These modifications must have worked, as the Imp went even better in the race and was so quick that it decimated its opposition with the fastest lap, it won the class and finished 11th overall. If this were not enough, it was a full 44 seconds ahead of Mike Freeman's second-placed Imp!

There was also a new face in the up-to-1-litre class: a certain hard-charging Formula 3 driver by the name of James Hunt was débuting in Jeremy Nightingale's Imp. He finished 29th!

Race 6 Silverstone 6 June 1970

At Silverstone, Bill McGovern was yet again fastest in practice and spectators were now becoming accustomed to the sight of an Imp much nearer the front of the grid than was reasonably expected. Lined up behind Bill were seven 1300 Minis, two more Imps, and three larger-engined Escorts. The Bevan Imp was also using the homologated Viva discs and Girling alloy callipers for the first time. These improved the stopping power enormously whilst giving a much better balance to the braking system.

TELEPHONE: 021-706 3371 TELEGRAMS: WONDER BIRMINGHAM	**GIRLING LIMITED** CHASSIS ENGINEERING		GBL 208943	INVOICE NUMBER		

SOLD TO:
G. Bevan.
63 Leesons Hill.
St.Pauls Cray.
ORPINGTON.
KENT.

CONSIGNED TO:

Kings Road,
TYSELEY,
BIRMINGHAM, 11.

FORM NO. 1061 T	DATE OF DESPATCH	PER	PACKED IN	PACKED BY	INVOICE DATE
	29. 5. 70.	P.P. 6/-			23/6/70

YOUR ORDER No.	OUR REFERENCE				
		64032678/9 O 12 R Caliper. @ £25-0s-0d per pair. paid by post accounts dept.	1-pair.	£25/0/0 per pair	25.0.0

£25 the pair...how times have changed.

The first practice went reasonably well, but even before the Imp was parked up in the paddock, George and Keith were hard at work changing the cam and exhaust system on the race engine. Times did not tumble during second practice therefore George was not happy. For the race he decided that they should abandon the race engine and fit the spare instead. The gear ratios were also changed (13.0, 8.8, 6.3, 5.3).

The spare engine must have been a good one, for in the race McGovern secured yet another fastest lap of 1:50.2 (in fact, he dipped under the existing lap record no less than five times during the race), the class win, fastest lap, lap record and 15th overall. McGovern crossed the line almost welded to the bootlid of Gordon Spice's Arden 1300 Cooper S, which was reputed to be producing around 130 bhp and, of course, was much lighter than the Imp.

One journalist was so impressed that he was moved to write:

...the astonishing McGovern made all the other 1000's look like snails chasing a hare!

One journalist's description was of snails chasing an hare!

Keith Tilbrook, Tom Simms and George, happy with life and soaking up the rays.

*The rapid Richard Longman could have been a serious contender for the Championship
had he not been sidelined by brake problems.*

The Bevan Imp was running like clockwork. Unfortunately, Richard Longman was less lucky when the servo on his Mini seized on solid—the resultant crash sidelining him for the rest of the season.

Race 7   Silverstone   27 June 1970
One of the criticisms quite justly levelled at the RAC series was the lack of variety, but come the next race meeting there would be no such criticism. Silverstone was playing host to the Tourist Trophy meeting, which was also the Fifth Round in the European Touring Car Challenge and Britain's contribution to this series. This was no sprint event, but a four-hour race split into two heats.

Continental competitors were a welcome addition and numerous 'foreign' cars swelled the grid—it was saloon car nirvana. Spectators at this meeting would have witnessed cars such as the Autodelta Alfa Romeo GTAms, Alpina BMW 2800 CSs, BMW 1600s, rotary-engined Mazda R100 Coupés and four Fiat Abarths, the latter hell bent on showing the Imps their propped-up bootlids!

Saloon car racing was made all the better by the inclusion of continental cars swelling the grids. Pictured is the Alfa Romeo GTAm of Nanni Galli during 1970 Tourist Trophy.

The Viva GT (below), an interloper in the series, but with Gerry Marshall at the wheel it was always a spectacular one.

Ostensibly, raising the bootlid on the tiny Fiats was to help expel hot air from the engine. However, when this was done, it was discovered that the little Fiat's aerodynamics improved and top speed on the quickest cars climbed by 6 mph. Carlo Abarth, the man behind the tiny Fiats—a master of homologation.

Other cars present included Gerry Marshall's Blydenstein-prepared Viva GT (pictured opposite), and Ford Deutschland's very desirable 2.4-litre Weslake-engined Capri 2300 GTs.

Driving Chris Craft's Broadspeed 1600 Escort in the first heat was Jackie Stewart. He would go on to take 4th overall and extract an impressive 9.3 mpg from his Escort in the process (not too tardy, as this figure is about the same as a 4.6-litre Range Rover currently achieves around town!).

Once again, Bill McGovern and the Bevan Imp, complete with a new engine and transaxle, was easily fastest in his class in practice, and in the race he shook off an early challenge from Woodman. Unfortunately, one of the Imp's rear tyres began to deflate so McGovern had to pit. The offending wheel would not budge, the wheel studs were hot and the nuts had welded themselves on. Precious minutes were lost as the team struggled to release them. With the tyre and

The amazing tiny Fiat Abarths—this one is driven by Ed Swan pictured at Brands Hatch.

wheel finally replaced, Bill was now some way behind and had to play 'Abarth catch-up'. One-by-one he picked them off, managing to pass the leading Abarth at Woodcote Corner on the last lap to finish 22nd overall in the first heat.

During the interval George set about changing the Imp's engine: it had not given any problems but he felt that a 'fresh' engine would keep the Imp to the fore. However, this was perceived to be a tad 'naughty' and not in the spirit of things. Quite justifiably this was protested and George had to refit the original engine.

Not that this mattered a jot of course. As if to prove a point, Bill made the Imp go even quicker in the second heat and finished an incredible 12th overall, secured fastest lap, won the class again and on aggregate ended in 16th place. All of the cars ahead of him possessed larger capacity engines; probably one more camshaft, 8 more valves, and some had approximately 400 bhp more! The icing on the cake though was the thrashing of the Abarths.

The Imp's engine was stripped after the finish—under the watchful eye of Des O'Dell, who had meandered over to have a look. Apparently, there was no wear evident, and George (and Des) pronounced the engine fit enough to run the race again.

Bill McGovern had really extended the Bevan Imp during these two races, but even he was surprised to discover just how quickly he had been going. According to the timekeeper's sheets the Bevan Imp was repeatedly timed at 136 mph down Silverstone's Hangar Straight—pretty impressive statistics for a 1-litre steel-bodied car.

The Imp's high top speed was a fact which always amazed Bill:

> Never once did I have to ease off to preserve the engine. George used to say that I could use it as hard as I liked. Often at the end of the race the tell-tale on the tachometer would read 10,400 rpm!

Bill had a thing about Silverstone and getting the gearing right. If the windsock was blowing in a certain direction, then he would insist that George change the gear ratios—he had obviously made the right decision for this race.

Before getting too euphoric about the Tourist Trophy result, it is worth remembering that luck was definitely on the Bevan Imp's side for this event. After all the European cars had been catered for, the RAC saw fit to accept only fourteen British entries. There is no doubting the fact that Bill McGovern and the Bevan Imp deserved the 16 points but with fewer UK-based competition perhaps they were not quite so hard won.

That said, the Bevan Imp had most comprehensively beaten the quickest Abarths. According to Doris Bevan's notes of the time, the rest of the one-litres—with the exception of Abarth number 2—were all considerably behind the Bevan Imp at the finish (*see table overleaf*).

Tourist Trophy

Positions of the other 1-litre cars – how far they were behind the Bevan Imp

Abarth No. 2	plus 1 sec
Abarth No. 4	plus 2 laps
Abarth No. 3	plus 3 laps
Abarth No. 1	plus 4 laps
Imp No. 2	plus 5 laps
Imp No. 3	plus 7 laps

Nice period shot captures R. Dystra's Fiat Abarth cornering hard in 1970 and taking the inside line of an Imp, which is closely followed by another of the Fiat Abarths.

Race 8   Croft   11 July 1970

A week after a practice session at Lydden the team were at Croft—a long haul.
Still, the effort, petrol and expenses paid off. Gerry Marshall and the Blydenstein
Viva GT added a welcome bit of diversity to the Group 2 scene.

After a very good practice session Gerry Marshall slotted the Vauxhall onto the second row of the grid. The Bevan Imp was only 4.6 seconds off the 2-litre Viva's pace but found itself on row seven, although it was easily the fastest 1-litre and a row ahead of Woodman in his Escort (which was now a 1300). Bill had worked the Bevan Imp very hard and managed to complete 52 practice laps and as a precaution the engine was changed for the race and the suspension was raised by a quarter of an inch. The gears were altered too (13.1, 8.5, 6.5, 5.5).

The race itself, held in two heats, was successful for the Bevan Imp, albeit uneventful. Woodman, who started from row eight, gave up an already unequal struggle when water found its way inside the bores of the Escort's engine—there was no class for steam-powered cars!

Despite a doughnut splitting in race one, Bill managed to get the class win, fastest lap, lap record and upset a lot of the larger-engined machinery as it scythed its way through the quality field to claim a magnificent 9th overall on aggregate.

Did the Bevan Imp ever have four wheels on the tarmac at any one time?

Race 9   Brands Hatch   18 July 1970

Home territory, Brands Hatch, British Grand Prix support race and champagne and garlands. It was fitting that it was here, at their 'local' circuit that the team clinched the Championship win due to their superb and consistent performances. With the best eight results system being in force, Bill McGovern could not be beaten and his second in class at Brands meant that his tally of 70 points was unmatchable. His closest rivals, Brian Muir and Frank Gardner, could only get a maximum of 68 (Australian, Frank Gardner, had won the Championship in 1967 and 1968 and went on to win the F5000 Championship in 1971 and 1972).

Brands Hatch was well used to the sight and angry sound of the Bevan Imp—though on this occasion it was not very kind to it. Why second, and not the usual class win? Well, in practice Bill was fastest as per usual, comfortably under his own lap record but George was somewhat dissatisfied with the Imp's performance and felt it wise to fit the spare engine for the race. The car was also fitted with new pads and tyres.

...and there goes that inside front wheel again! (was it a victory wave, perhaps?)

The race itself was a rather fraught affair. Possibly due to championship stress, the usually impeccably reliable Imp played up on the start line, and, to his horror Bill found the car gearless, due to a faulty selector fork. When the entire field had departed, he was able to roll the car downhill, snick into first gear and away he went. Suitably fired up, by the sixth lap he had already passed Freeman, but by the half-distance point another one of the rear tyres began to deflate. Thankfully, the tyre remained partially inflated and stayed on the rim as Bill fought to overcome this handicap on his way to second place in class, fastest lap and yet another lap record. John Fitzpatrick had wrung the neck of his Escort GT on his way to a magnificent fourth overall, whilst James Hunt was less successful. Driving Jeremy Nightingale's Imp his race was terminated by a coupling failure.

The pundits had been proved right—the 1970 Champion had come from the 1-litre class and he had been driving an Imp. Bets were being taken for a repeat win in 1971 although the odds were not as long as they had once been. While the Bevan camp were enjoying their celebratory tea and biscuits, Jochen Rindt took the chequered flag in the Grand Prix in a Lotus 72C

Clubbing

Despite having won the Championship, instead of packing up and resting on its laurels, the team decided to contest the remaining rounds plus a club event at Brands for good measure. For the 'clubbie' George could experiment a bit. The Imp was fitted with a five-speed Jack Knight transaxle using 16.0, 9.7, 7.15, 6.5 5.7 gears, small spacers were placed under the rear springs, the front camber was tweaked to half a degree negative and 7-inch front and 8-inch rear rims were used (both fitted with 4.75 x 10 tyres). These modifications must have worked as the Imp was fastest in practice, it equalled the lap record and it won the race (which was stopped during lap 7 because of an accident).

Race 10   Oulton Park   22 August 1970

At Oulton, the car had to be reunited with its normal four-speed transaxle. 7-inch front and 8-inch rear wheels were fitted with 4.75 x 11.50 tyres. George tweaked the front camber to 1.5 degrees negative and fitted spacers under the rear springs to increase the ride height a touch.

During the race, Bill saw and smelt smoke inside the cabin, and called into the pits to have a possible oil leak investigated. Indeed, oil was leaking from the cambox gasket and dripping onto the hot exhaust. George checked the car over, nipped up the cambox bolts and gave the car the okay. Bill got back into the race and although well behind, he did manage to haul the Imp up to a 2nd in class, 17th overall, fastest lap and claiming a lap record in the process. George made a note that on the next visit to Oulton second gear should be changed from 8.8.1 to 8.5.1.

Race 11   Brands Hatch   31 August 1970

The 'Guards Trophy' meeting. George's meticulous pre-race inspection routine did not throw up any horror stories; the only thing that needed doing was to change the rear brake shoes. But ever keen to 'up the pace', he also changed the ratios (16.0, 8.5, 6.5 and 5.5).

Brands Hatch was home to the final round in the Championship and Bill appeared to throw caution to the wind. He qualified on the 6th row of the grid, alongside much more powerful cars putting in a time of 1:51.4—which was inside the lap record!

The race was run in two heats. At the head of the field in heat one there were a number of incidents. Fortunately, McGovern managed to avoid the carnage (although the engine suffered from some oil surge later in the race which was a bit of a worry). Another good drive in heat two saw him net 15th overall on aggregate, the class win, fastest lap and lap record (only 2.38 mph slower than Fitzpatrick's 1300 Escort).

"Right Bill, I want you to pass all the 1300 Escorts—and a couple of 1600s for good measure!"

Bill makes the Imp as wide as possible. (Note the damage to the spats).

No Peace for the Wicked (Imp)! [1]

At last, it was time for the Bevan Imp to have a bit of a breather, although it was wheeled out on the 3rd December for *Motor* magazine's Michael Bowler to have a spin around Silverstone's short circuit.

Bowler was very impressed. Despite the fact that it was an extremely wet day and the circuit was awash, his best lap time was a commendable 1:17.0. Bill, observing from the pits was astounded by how 'angry' their Imp sounded—it was the first occasion where he had been able to see and hear the Imp in action.

George, Bill and the Imp then visited Brands Hatch no fewer than five times before the 1971 season commenced, focussing on getting the suspension set-up and tyre choice absolutely spot-on for their second crack at the Championship. Interestingly, on two of these occasions, the Imp was fitted with a long-stroke 1092 cc engine that George was experimenting with.

Mean, moody ...and magnificent!

Table of Placings 1970 (11 rounds)				
Class Wins	Class Seconds	Lap Records	Fastest Laps	Top Ten Places
8	2	6	11	1 (9th)

CHAPTER **5**

1971 and all that

THE team approached the 1971 season feeling decidedly upbeat; George and Bill reasoned that if they could win the championship (now referred to as the RAC Group 2 Touring Car Championship) once, then what could stop them winning it again. Could they? Would they?

Whilst others had been 'potting-up' their seedlings George had been busy in his garden shed, not raising flowers, but raising power! He had managed to liberate some more torque and an extra 2 bhp from the Imp's engine, which now boasted 112 Bevan horses—this was probably due to the fitment of a Fraser race camshaft and some Peter Bevan magic.

George happy and contented at work in his 'powerhouse'.

For the 1971 season, Bill McGovern was reunited with his 1970 car. The car itself received very little attention. Apart from a thorough once-over, a subtle reworking of the rear suspension to cope with George's penchant for fitting it with the widest tyres possible, everything else was left untouched. This made good sense really, as George felt it unlikely that any of his competitors would have made sufficient progress over the winter months to offer a serious challenge. Confident yes, but George was certainly not complacent, because he had also built four spare engines—and even a spare Imp!

Snapshot of the Imp twins at camp!

The spare Imp is a bit of a mystery. The thinking in some quarters is that this car was built up from a rallycross shell donated by no less a person than Des O'Dell. This story does seem rather difficult to swallow bearing in mind the oft-fractious relationship between Des and George. However, if it was this shell, then it is very likely that it had previously been home to a Lynton twin-cam rallycross engine when the Competition Department were trying it back-to-back against a full-race single cam Imp (which was quicker by the way). Anyway, wherever the shell was obtained from, it was stripped and rebuilt into a Bevan Imp replica. It was, in fact, identical to the original car and although it went well, it was very heavy and always circulated at around a second a lap slower than the original Bevan Imp.

Sadly, Keith Tilbrook had been badly injured in a road accident and was unable to assist with the mechanical work. To keep the Bevan Imp at the front of the pack during 1971, George had something of an entourage accompanying him as he had enlisted the help of Tom Simms, Norman Winn and Royston Paskins. Tom was in charge of all things electrical, and Norman Winn (who had worked in the Rootes Competition Department and was Alan Fraser's chief mechanic in the Fraser Imp days) and Royston Paskins kept the Imp running, helped to build the engines and prepared the cars with George. Royston Paskins actually worked for George on a day-to-day basis. In addition to his car-related workload, on a few occasions he remembers also having to help George and Peter sort out problems with the Chinese cookers!

The RAC in the meantime had upped the ante. For 1971 it would be the best nine results of the season that would count towards the Championship, one more than in 1970.

In spite of the pressure of preparing the Imps and keeping an eye on the family business, George and Royston had found time to build some Imp race engines for favoured customers. Pauli Toivonen had popped over to collect a fresh 'Bevan' Imp engine in readiness for his assault on the 1971 Finnish Ice Racing Championship, as had Juhani Kynsilehto (the pair had been cleaning up in Finnish races in their 'Bevan' Imps, Pauli finishing first and Juhani second in the Finnish Championship in this year).

Race 1   Brands Hatch   21 March 1971
The first race was at the team's favourite circuit, Brands Hatch, and was run in two 20 lap heats. The season started well for Bill McGovern. However, newcomer and class rival, Melvyn Adams, running on the proverbial shoestring (using Bevan Imp cast-offs), looked as if he could mount an occasional threat as the season progressed.

Melvyn Adams Imp keeps ahead of Adrian Webb's similar car.

In the wet practice Bill showed his intent by posting a 1:50.4. Those who harboured the notion that they could win the 1971 Championship had no doubt that they going to have work very hard indeed. This lap time was just a smidgen slower than Rod Mansfield's muscular RS1600 and just outside Bill's own lap record set on a dry track! Rapid Mini man, Mo Mendham, well used to battling it out with hot Imps in club races, had wrestled his Cooper 'S' to a good 1:52.8, ahead of all the other Minis and some of the Escorts. Barrie 'Whizzo' Williams was on row 7 with a 1:54.1 in his Cooper 'S'. Back on Row 9, but adding some welcome glamour to the line-up, was Jean Denton in her Imp with a 2:05.8.

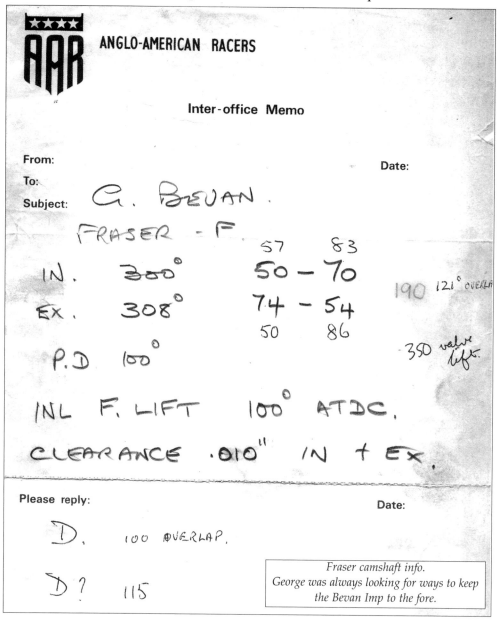

Fraser camshaft info.
George was always looking for ways to keep
the Bevan Imp to the fore.

To up the pace, the Bevan Imp's gearing had been altered to 13.6, 7.8, 6.3 and 5.3. and to ensure that it stayed on the black stuff, George had somehow managed to shoehorn a set of 11.6-inch wide tyres under the rear arches.

The 'improvements' must have worked because Bill screamed his way to 11th overall in the first heat. Mo Mendham, keeping the Imp in sight at first, spun and then rolled his Mini—fortunately walking away unhurt. New class rival, Melvyn Adams, was going well in his well-turned out Imp but, unfortunately, his engine put a rod through the block and his race, like his engine, was run. Jean Denton also retired.

In the second heat, with both Melvyn and Mo sidelined, Bill bagged another class win, fastest lap and finished 11th on aggregate, just behind Martin Thomas's thundering 5.7-litre Camaro! John Turner finished second in class and in 21st place.

Compared with the previous year's season opener at Brands Hatch, this one was a walkover. Would the run of good form continue?

Race 2   Oulton Park   9 April 1971

Whilst the rest of the Championship circus hot tailed it to Snetterton in Norfolk, the up to 1000 cc and 1001-1300 competitors went to Oulton Park instead. It was not easy getting entries though. It seemed that if you ran in the small capacity classes, then places in the RAC Championship rounds were hard to come by. As reigning Champion, Bill McGovern had no such problems though, his entry was guaranteed.

Bill kept most of the Escorts at bay.

In practice, Bill reduced his lap record and as third fastest overall found himself on the front row, much to the displeasure of Chrysler Competition boss, Des O'Dell. Why? Well, Chrysler test driver and former Fraser racer, Bernard Unett, was behind him on row 2 in the Works Imp! Woodman had slotted his 1.3 GT Escort alongside the Bevan Imp.

Woodman got the drop at the start and led until fate dealt him yet another cruel blow; a selector broke handing the lead to Dave Matthews in another Escort 1.3 GT. Woodman's selector had collapsed because his team was forced into using an old part. A strike at Ford meant that no new gearbox components had been available.

Although Dave Matthew's won in his Broadspeed Escort, Bill drove an outstanding race. Despite the Imp's 300 ccs deficit he achieved a magnificent 2nd place overall, class win and the fastest lap.

Dave Matthews Escort was almost always the class of the 1300 field.

In Between (going round in circles)

Even with his busy schedule, Bill McGovern found time to try his hand at stadium racing. He was reunited with Paul Emery and drove Emery's Hot Rod Imp in what the press described as a very 'physical' race. Bill adapted to his new steed and the slippery surface very well, 'forcing' his way through to take second overall at the White City track.

Race 3   Thruxton   12 April 1971

After first practice, problems with gear selection meant that the team had no option other than to change the Imp's gearbox. At Thruxton the 1-litre class was a hotbed of talent and even Bill McGovern would have his work cut out in keeping the Bevan Imp to the fore.

Unett was using Jean Denton's Works-prepared Imp because Jean had managed to lose her road licence, and as such was ineligible to race. The car went well, although its suspension was not yet fully sorted, due to the uncertainty as to the car's future. Other competition for Bill McGovern came in the form of the Guy Automobile Engineering Imp driven by quick Imp man, John Turner. This car was bucking the Weber DCOE trend as its engine used a pair of Dellorto DHLA carburettors. George had experimented with Dellortos although he had decided to stick with Webers on the Bevan Imp. Some tuners swore by Dellortos, whilst others swore at them! When set up properly they work very well indeed, producing a good spread of torque, which may go some way towards accounting for the Guy Automobile Imp's surprising turn of speed.

A Rotoflex coupling failure, that age old Imp Achilles' heel, ruined a very good race for the Bevan Imp. Before the Rotoflex coupling had parted company from the driveshaft the car had been absolutely flying. Bill had stormed through the field and latched the Imp on to the rear of the very fastest 1300 Fords. Before his untimely retirement he had managed the fastest lap and a new lap record—some small consolation for all his effort.

The view the opposition invariably got!

Ice supremo Juhani Kynsilehto was also trying out his new Bevan-engined Imp at Thruxton. Unfortunately, luck was not on his side when his Imp lost a wheel causing a huge three-wheel moment and subsequent retirement.

Race 4   Silverstone   8 May 1971

The Bevan Imp was on the fourth row of the grid at Silverstone, sandwiched between Terry Drury's rebuilt RS1600 and last year's 1-litre sparring partner, Vince Woodman, in his Escort 1.3 GT. The Bevan Imp still reigned supreme in its class. George, never one to rest on his laurels, did all he could to keep the car in front.

For practice the team trialled a 'hot' new specification of engine but Doris Bevan's stopwatch showed that it gave no significant improvement. For the race George decided that it would be prudent to revert to the original, and tried and tested engine specification. Bill ran the race engine in during the second practice session and on lap 21 he pitted for new tyres.

In the race proper, McGovern pulled out all the stops and was the class master, harrying larger-engined cars on his way to getting another class win, fastest in class and 15th overall.

Living up to his early season promise, and second in class, was the hard-charging and ever-improving Melvyn Adams.

Time for more team talk.

Race 5   Crystal Palace   31 May 1971

At Crystal palace, the organisers decided to split the meeting into two separate parts. One race featured the under 1300s, and the other, the larger capacity cars. The Bevan team had the wind put up them a little when in practice they discovered that John Turner's Imp was only 0.4 of a second behind (Turner had previously won the Osram GEC and Atlantic Saloon Car titles).

Bill McGovern, after the practice session upset, proved dominant during the actual race.

Turner's pace provided the cue for some frantic work in the Bevan camp. The gear ratios were raised a touch, but this was to prove unnecessary because the luckless Turner did not manage one complete lap in the race due to mechanical problems.

Gears were on the agenda for Melvyn Adams too. He had a reoccurrence of the transmission problems that had beset him earlier in the season. As a result he was forced to keep his Imp in 3rd gear for the duration of the race. The enormous stress this placed on the engine caused the oil pressure to drop, and in order to keep all of his Imp's 998 ccs in one piece, Melvyn was forced to slow towards the end. McGovern, untroubled by any such problems, threw the Imp around the track and notched up yet another class win, fastest lap, lap record and a stunning 2nd overall. Incredibly, for 23 of the 25 laps, Bill's times only varied by nine hundredths of a second—such was his incredible consistency.

Race 6   Silverstone   5 June 1971

Silverstone, and a new type of racing tyre was fitted to the Imp. Even more grip resulted in yet even more forceful driving from McGovern.

Norman Winn talks to Bill, while Doris Bevan jots down the times (she was incredibly accurate).

The grippy Imp was hardly ever on four wheels; three-wheeling became its norm, with the odd two-wheel 'moment' thrown in for good measure! Perhaps McGovern was trying too hard. While blasting his way through the pack the Bevan Imp clipped the rear of Brian Peacock's 1300 Escort as it slowed prematurely. The seemingly minor impact caused the Imp's special front-mounted oil/water radiator to rupture and the subsequent loss of fluids brought about the car's demise on lap 6. John Turner, always in contention, grasped the mettle and flew through to take the win from Melvyn Adams and Adrian Webb. The disconsolate McGovern pitted to find he had nailed the fastest lap—a small consolation.

Six races, two retirements (one through component failure, and one through a very rare driver error). George and Bill were secretly blessing the RAC's decision to stage the Championship over 12 rounds in this year, with the best 9 counting.

Race 7   Croft   9 July 1971

It was a depleted Championship circus that arrived at Croft circuit, with only 17 cars having made the effort to get there. Croft is a demanding circuit and more of a power course than it first appears. The team needed to put the two previous disappointments behind it and Bill had put a serious amount of practice miles in to ensure that the Bevan Imp was fit and feisty.

Bill McGovern keeping it really tight.

After some experimentation during a very hard practice session, George had decided that 13.6, 7.8, 6.3, 5.3, were the ideal Croft 'cogs'. On this tight and challenging track, McGovern easily led the class in practice and was well on the pace. In the race he started from the fourth row of the grid and in an uneventful race for him, dispatching Richard Ellis' Escort 1.3 GT on his way to another class win, fastest lap and lap record. Well behind in second place was Melvyn Adams in Tony Charnell's Imp—Melvyn's Imp had not been ready in time.

Incidentally, as a reward for all its hard work, the team took home two trophies, one barometer and £6 in cash!

Mr Consistency
To give some idea of Bill's uncanny ability to turn in almost identical times lap after lap, the chart on the following page lists each lap at Croft.

Lap	Time	Lap	Time	Lap	Time	Lap	Time	Lap	Time
1	71.02	6	63.05	11	63.02	16	63.03	21	63.02
2	63.09	7	63.04	12	63.01	17	63.06	22	63.00
3	63.05	8	63.00	13	63.00	18	62.08	23	63.02
4	62.09	9	62.09	14	63.03	19	63.03	24	62.09
5	63.06	10	63.02	15	63.02	20	63.04	25	63.05

McGovern signals his winning wave.

Race 8   Silverstone   17 July 1971

This was the British Grand Prix support feature. Unlike the previous year, Bill arrived at Silverstone as a contender, not as leader. He was trailing way behind the Championship leader, Brian Muir, who had already managed to amass 66 points in his explosively powerful Camaro, to Bill's 54.

George knew that something had to be done if the Bevan Imp was to close this gap and stand any chance of winning the series title. After practice, the gear ratios were changed once again (13.6, 7.8, 6.0, 5.05) in an attempt to raise the Imp's top speed.

There were some welcome new faces and sparring partners at Silverstone. Martino Finotto was in the Jolly Club Alfa Romeo GTAJ, and top club racer, Dave Brodie, was there in his familiar Escort. Brodie's Escort had been hastily converted to Group 2 specification and he finished 18th in the race. Vince Woodman was wondering if his run of bad luck would ever end: during practice his engine had put a rod through the block and 'team orders' meant that the unfortunate Teddy Savory had to 'donate' the engine from his car.

McGovern and Finotto battled throughout the whole race, Finotto (with 160 bhp at his disposal) just getting the upper hand in 13th place, with McGovern seemingly bolted to his bumper in 14th. McGovern won the class from Melvyn Adams getting the lap record in the process, dropping it from 1.50.2 to a 1.49.8.

Ralph Broad, who was not amused by the Imp's searing pace—and the fact that it led most of the more powerful 1300 Escorts home, protested the car. Pit lane rumour was that the Imp's engine was a special large capacity one—figures as high as 1140 cc were being bandied about. Of course, after the obligatory strip down, the engine was pronounced to be a perfectly legal 998 cc. The whole pointless exercise just wasted time, a set of expensive Wills rings and caused unnecessary bad feelings. George and Bill did not require a 'big' engine to beat the Escorts—the small one was perfectly adequate!

While the Bevan Imp was having its 'internal', Jackie Stewart took the Grand Prix honours in a Tyrell 003.

Vince Woodman as usual pushing hard in his 1300 GT Escort.

Race 9   Oulton Park   21 August 1971

The Oulton Park meeting saw the Imp 0.6 seconds under the class lap record and on the fourth row of the grid. In the second practice, McGovern had uncharacteristically missed a gear and over-revved the engine (12,000 rpm was indicated on the tell-tale!). Amazingly, the engine stayed together, but as a precaution, George elected to dig out the spare engine and fit it for the race.

The spare (998 cc!) engine proved to be a 'good-un', and McGovern quickly dispensed with all the 1-litre contenders and then found himself battling with Bill Mowatt's 1.3 Mini. When the Mini slowed towards the end, Bill nipped past into 9th place. Behind this race-long skirmish, Melvyn Adams and Peter Baldwin (1.3 Mini) were also keeping the crowd on its toes. This pair was having a terrific scrap, which was resolved in Baldwin's favour when Adams spun at Lodge and slipped down the order. McGovern won the class from a recovering Adams and popped another fastest lap on to the score sheets for good measure.

Race 10   Brands Hatch   30 August 1971

Things seemed to be turning a little sour in the Championship. Not only were there fresh complaints that the racing had become too processional, but far too many cars were dropping out through mechanical failure. This was not music to the ears of the RAC. The British Saloon Car Series was, after all, the country's premier Saloon Car Championship, surely more cars could manage to make it across the finish line?

Bill McGovern had been clawing his way up the points table and the gap between him and Muir was closing. There was no time for complacency though, and despite Race 10 being at their 'local', Brands Hatch, even the typically calm and confident George Bevan was getting jittery. To settle collective nerves the Bevan Imp had been fitted with a fresh and very carefully built engine, which Bill had gently run-in during practice. During the second practice session a lack of grip saw Bill pit for new tyres.

Incredibly, he was also six seconds a lap faster than all the other Imps, who were sulking way back on the eighth row.

In the cool and damp conditions, the Imp's engine breathed more deeply and provided lungfuls of power. Whilst others tiptoed, Bill danced the Imp around the slippery track and got the customary fastest lap, class win, and a stupendous 10th overall. He could not relax though, and due to another suspect Rotoflex coupling (racing slicks and extreme driveshaft angles put as much strain on these components in one race as a lifetime of normal driving would have done) sending warning vibrations through the drivetrain; he was forced to ease the pace towards the end. There were only two other finishers in the class. Adams was second.

Out Testing

Following race 10, the team were out at Brands Hatch testing both the spare car (with the intention of using it in 1972) and trying out another long-stroke engine (1098 cc this time) and a new design of driveshaft. The original car was also there getting some laps in, but using a 998 cc engine.

Race 11 Mallory Park 26 September 1971

The Brands result had done wonders for the team's confidence. McGovern had closed the gap on rival Muir and when he arrived at Mallory for the penultimate round, things looked much rosier for the Championship. The twisty Leicestershire circuit suited both the Imp and Bill McGovern, as did the weather— foggy and wet. Another class win would place the title in McGovern's grasp for a second time.

Bill and George looking determined and confident. A winning combination.

With so much at stake you would have thought that he would have exercised a little caution, but caution is not a word that is in Bill McGovern's vocabulary. Unusually, for him, he set off like a scalded cat, quickly establishing himself near the front of the pack in this the up-to-1000 cc and 1001-to-1300 feature race. Some seriously quick cars were entered, but Bill quickly shook off all his small-capacity pursuers and badgered the larger capacity cars on his route to the fastest lap, the class win and a 6th overall. This was Bill's ninth class win of the year, and his points tally was now beyond the reach of his nearest rivals, Brian Muir in the Wiggins Teape Camaro, and Dave Matthews in the Broadspeed Escort 1.3 GT.

The Bevan team, therefore, and quite incredibly, took the Championship for the second successive year. As they retired to the caravan for a celebratory drink, George and Bill were already discussing the very real possibility of a hat trick.

Running-in, please pass—while you can!

George had fitted a new engine to Bevan Imp number one and, eight days before the Motor Show 200 event, the team were at Brands testing out the car and running in a new engine. George saw fit to change the rear springs and fit $3^1/2$-inch Aeon rubber spring assisters.

Race 12   Brands Hatch   24 October 1971

The BARC Motor Show 200 meeting promised to be a good one, as typically it attracted a large number of continental entries. There were representatives from Sweden, Holland, Finland and Denmark. The Danish entry included the Imps of Paul Lund and Jorgen Kofoed (who managed to total the rear of his Imp in practice, due to a backwards off-track excursion at Clearways).

The pressure was off Bill and it clearly showed. In practice, and using a new engine, he posted an astonishing 1.49.2, a full 2 seconds below the lap record, although one driveshaft almost exited stage left in the process! There was quite a bit of playing around with the Imp's specification at this event too. The gearing was altered yet again (13.6, 7.8. 6.3 and 5.3), the rear springs were changed and Aeon progressive rubber bump stops were fitted. Remarkably, considering the depth of talent and machinery at this event, McGovern found himself and the little Imp sharing the sixth row, right alongside Zekia Redjep's lusty RS1600.

In the race, Bill slaughtered the lap record (down to 1.49.9), got fastest lap, the class win from Adams and 13th overall, a magnificent end to a hard-fought season. Although it was not the end for the hard-worked Imp.

Tragically, the day was marred by the death of Jo Siffert in the end-of-season Victory Race. His BRM P160 crashed at Hawthorn Hill, the fastest section of the circuit, following a suspension breakage.The car burst into flames and Siffert, who had suffered no more than a fractured leg on impact, died of asphyxia.

Table of Placings 1971 (12 rounds)				
Class Wins	Class Seconds	Lap Records	Fastest Laps	Top Ten Places
10	–	5	13	1 x 10th
				2 x 2nd (up-to-1300)
				1 x 6th (up-to-1300)

Page from Autosport *magazine 2 October 1971*

No Peace for the Wicked (Imp)! [2]

The following weekend the team were again at Brands testing the Imp, which was fitted with yet another new engine but this one was equipped with one of the very rare Coventry Climax (probably an ex-Fraser one) 'deep' cylinder heads and 9.5-inch wide rear wheels. Exactly a week later they competed in the BRSCC organised Hepolite-Glacier Championship Special Saloon event at Brands Hatch on the short circuit. As if to emphasise the fact that the Bevan Imp was the fastest 1-litre car in the country, Bill McGovern destroyed all the opposition—which included three other very quick Imps, Les Nash's Anglia and a host of 1300 cc Minis—and was duly rewarded with 1st overall and a new lap record (56 seconds), which was 1.6 seconds under the existing record (*see race sheet below*).

On the 8th December they were back at Brands with the Championship-winning car, which was now sporting anti-roll bars front and rear (and still equipped with the deep head). On lap 3 the Imp pitted for a plug change and on lap 11 George removed the rear spring spacers and changed the main jets from 130 to 120. Bill, unhappy with the car, pitted on lap 16 for the plugs to be checked and the ignition advanced. After all this fettling the Imp could only manage a 57.1, slower than had been hoped for, but nevertheless, still impressive.

With the Christmas pudding barely settled in their stomachs, the team was off to Brands Hatch on the 27th December for the post

British Racing and Sports Car Club Limited

Empire House Chiswick High Road London W. 4.

TELEPHONE: Area Code 01-995 0345/6/7   TELEGRAPHIC ADDRESS: CARACE, LONDON, W.4.

RACE INFORMATION

CLOSED RACE MEETING - BRANDS HATCH

SUNDAY, 31st OCTOBER, 1971

INFORMATION SHEET NO: 7   PRACTICE TIMES

Weather Conditions: Sunny, track dry

HEPOLITE-GLACIER CHAMPIONSHIP RACE 'B' - For Special Saloon Cars.

No.	Driver	Car	Time M S	Speed m.p.h.
139	Bill McGovern	Sunbeam Imp	56.0	79.71
143	Les Nash	Ford Anglia 105E	57.2	
138	Ray Calcutt	Hillman Imp	57.4	
136	Jeff Ward	Hillman Imp	58.0	
137	Alex Clacher	Hillman Imp	58.8	
135	David Hipperson	BLMC Mini-Cooper 'S'	59.0	
142	John Hipkiss	BLMC Mini	59.0	
146	Paul Harmer	BLMC Mini-Cooper 'S'	59.2	
151	Paul Butler	BLMC Mini-Cooper 'S'	59.2	
154	Mike Darrieulat	BLMC Mini-Cooper 'S'	59.6	
144	Jenny Dell	BLMC Mini-Clubman	1 00.4	
150	John Schneider	BLMC Mini-Cooper 'S'	1 00.6	
132	Glen Pennefather	BLMC Mini-Cooper 'S'	1 01.2	
133	Paul Reynolds	BLMC Mini-Cooper 'S'	1 01.4	
134	Micki Vandervell	BLMC Mini-Cooper 'S'	1 02.4	
131	Dave Phillips	BLMC Mini-Cooper 'S'	1 02.6	
148	Paddy O'Donnell	BLMC Mini	1 05.4	
147	Gerald Hulford	BLMC Mini	1 07.6	

Christmas BRSCC meeting. After breaking the gear lever and having to have a gearbox change during the wet practice, the Imp went on to win on a drying track.

Finally, the Imp could now be put under covers until the start of the 1972 season in March.

CHAPTER **6**

1972 and all that

FOR 1972, the Championship had secured sponsorship from paper merchants, Wiggins Teape (who had been very active during 1971) and it was renamed the 'Wiggins Teape Paperchase British Saloon Car Championship'. It would be run to FIA Appendix 'J' (1972) Group 2 regulations over 10 rounds. As a result, the 1600 cc class was no more and the class divisions were now 0-1000 cc, 1001-1300 cc, 1301-2000 cc, and over 2000 cc. In the Escort camp much time was spent 'stretching' the 1600 cc cars to around 1800 cc—some would end the season as 2-litres.

Also new was the fact that each competitor was now allotted a permanent number. To reward drivers, others than those winning, Wiggins Teape introduced a much-welcomed incentive scheme, with prizes being awarded during and at the end of the season.

It was felt that the 1972 Championship would be an absolute cracker and the keyword for the season was 'more'. There was 'more' prize money, 'more' variety, 'more' large capacity machinery—and 'more' stress, because there were fewer opportunities to bag points. With only 10 rounds in place of the previous year's 12 rounds, and the best 7 results counting, competition would be intense.

Bill and George sitting in the country's Number 1 racing saloon car.

There was the inevitable pre-season banter and the motoring press were almost universal in their predictions. The word was, at least another class title for the McGovern/Bevan combo—much being made of Bill's driving, the Imp's remarkable speed and George's exemplary preparation.

However, it was Vince Woodman who was emerging as the bookies' favourite for the overall Championship title. He was a smooth and extremely fast driver who really deserved to do well. Dave Matthews, another supremely quick driver, could also mount a serious challenge.

In Class D (up-to-1-litre) it was thought that Mo Mendham and his Mini Cooper would also give Bill a run for his money. Mo concurred with this prediction and fully expected to beat Bill, but in the event, despite some stirring drives on Mendham's part, this did not quite happen.

There were a number of other Imps entered in the Championship, for Melvyn Adams, Adrian Webb, Terry Watts, Trevor Wilcox and Ivor Goodwin. Goodwin had forsaken his Mini for an Imp and purchased John Turner's Guy Automobiles example.

The new regulations had also ruled out lightweight bonnets, boots, doors, plastic windows and removal of the bumpers, (although the RAC was expected to allow the fitment of plastic windows and the removal of bumpers for some races).

Not much had been done to the double Championship-winning Bevan Imp over the winter months, although a fair amount of George's time had been spent beavering away in his beloved garden shed. He had been intent on extracting as much power and reliability from the Imp engine as was possible. The 1972-specification engine boasted a modified exhaust manifold, a wild Fraser camshaft and some cylinder head mods.

Bill was delighted to discover that he now had a vigorous 116 bhp at his disposal. He felt that this hike in power and improvements in driveability should enable him to dispatch all of the 1-litres. In fact, pre-season testing had demonstrated that the Bevan Imp would probably be quicker than most of the 1300 front-runners.

To ensure that the team were fully prepared, George and Royston had also been busy building another spare car, the 'original' spare having been sold, (memories have dimmed over time, but it is thought to have been purchased by German racer, Hans Sauer).

Tyres were a fascination to George and he had always ensured that the Imp was fitted the widest set of 'boots' practicable, and this year was no exception. After the first couple of races the team intended to use the recently introduced Dunlop 570 slick tyres. George had failed in his attempt to squeeze a super-wide set of these under the Imp's flared metal arches and had to relent and fit the wider fibreglass Group 2 'works' items.

1972 saw the debut of the front airdam, which would be used as and when George thought necessary. When this was first used on the Bevan Imp it worked well, but it also prevented air from passing beneath the car and cooling the transaxle. To cool the 'cogs,' George fabricated a scoop into the airdam and from the scoop he ran cold air ducting all the way to the transaxle.

Clubbing

This BRSCC organised event at Brands Hatch was the season opener. Bill McGovern and the Bevan Imp contested this event and showed onlookers and the other competitors exactly what it could do. Although the Imp could only manage to get off the line in second place, by the flag it was 10 seconds ahead of the second-placed 1300 Cooper 'S', driven by Terry Harmer. In the second race the Imp triumphed yet again with Terry Harmer taking another second place.

Race 1   Brands Hatch   19 March 1972

If practice was anything to go by, then things were looking good for this 'Race of Champions'. Jonathan Buncombe, a deceptively quick driver, was also on the pace. His Richard Longman-powered Mini was flying (despite having to run the engine in during practice), it was easily fastest of all the 1300s. Richard Longman's tuning concern had really started to extract some serious power and torque from the 5-port Mini engine.

Jonathan Buncombe and Vince Woodman—great mates, great rivals.

The Bevan Imp was unquestionably the quickest 1-litre in practice: just seven tenths of a second behind Buncombe's lighter, and more powerful, 5-port headed Mini.

Bill drove a clean and tidy race passing Rob Mason's Mini Cooper to take the class win, fastest lap and 8th overall, ahead of Melvyn Adams. Adams' season had started badly because he had to contend with a misfiring engine.

The new RAC regulations had obviously had a detrimental effect on a number of the other runners, who were seemingly suffering from the extra weight they were carrying. A top ten finish in the first race boded well for Bill McGovern.

Follow the leader!

Eighth overall was a cracking start to the season and the bookies' odds began to shift from Woodman to McGovern. If their early season form was anything to go by, Bill and the Imp looked set to take the Championship for an absolutely incredible and unprecedented third time.

Race 2   Oulton Park   31 March 1972

During the practice sessions George decided to experiment with the Imp's shock absorber settings and he adjusted them to suit the wet conditions.

Bill was again quickest of the 1-litres, but was surprised to find himself some 2.6 seconds off the pace of the fastest Mini, which was expertly piloted by Mike Drinkwater. The Mini's traction was seemingly superior to the Imp's, but despite this upset the Bevan Imp still went extremely well at Oulton Park, mixing it with the larger capacity cars, giving most of the 1300 Cooper S's a hard time and getting the customary class win.

Bill did not quite have it all his own way though, because the experienced and quick Mendham had lived up to his pre-season promise, and finished second in class. What is more, in the process he had snatched the fastest lap from a surprised McGovern, although McGovern ended up two places ahead of Mendham in 12th.

Race 3   Thruxton   3 April 1972

Quick Imper, Melvyn Adams, had something to prove. He had been very busy tweaking his car, and at Thruxton he used his self-prepared engine and full-race gearbox (which was new for this season) to very good effect.

In practice Melvyn's nicely prepared, but budget Imp was significantly faster than the 'all-singing, all dancing' Bevan version. This was not the done thing at all, and Adam's blistering pace caught the Bevan equipe with their collective trousers down! Understandably, George was not having any of this and he and his team set too and changed the race engine's camshaft for an even peakier one and swapped the transaxle ratios as well.

Melvyn Adams went very well—despite using Bevan cast-offs.

Come race day, the weather was cold and windy. McGovern ran the engine in during the first part of the race and when it had 'loosened up' he gritted his teeth and floored the throttle. In the process he got his lap times to 1.6 seconds below Adams's best, and the Imp began to mix it with Teddy Savory's VWM Motors' 1300 GT Escort and Chris Montague's Cooper 'S', swapping places with the Mini continually.

The final result was a class win, fastest lap and a stunning 9th overall. The determined Adams was second in class in 12th place, and Mendham not far behind in 14th.

So, Race 3 and another giant-slaying top ten finish! Who could stop the Bevan Imp's race to the title?

Race 4   Silverstone   21 April 1972

The BRDC organised Silverstone meeting saw Bill's good form continue. The Bevan Imp was some four seconds quicker than the rest of the class in practice and the same time as Chris Montague and his Mini Cooper 'S'. Bill's fastest lap of 1:52.7 was good but still a long way off his record, which stood at 1:49.8.

Whilst things were going smoothly for Bill in the up-to-1-litre class, in the 1300 class things were a little more fraught. An uncharacteristic spin by Vince Woodman led him to be clouted by his good friend and close rival Buncombe. Woodman continued and Buncombe pitted, but after a quick inspection of the damage felt able to continue. However, eventually Buncombe would retire with a puncture.

The Bevan Imp's progress may have been smooth, but Bill was not having things all his own way. He and Montague traded places throughout the race, with the Imp just managing to squeeze ahead by 0.1 seconds at the end. Melvyn Adams was not far behind in second place until he was unfortunately baulked by Gordon Dawkins's Cooper 'S', which slowed him, allowing Andrew Webb's Imp to get

past and grab 2nd place. Bill was well ahead by now and untroubled by the scuffle going on behind him, he disappeared into the distance to take 16th overall, and another class win and the fastest lap.

"Now George, what you really need is a nice Mini!"
Paddy Hopkirk (right) chatting to George Bevan.

Bill McGovern now tied for the overall Championship lead with Dave Matthews and his 1.8-litre Escort RS—both having won their class each time out.

Race 5   Crystal Palace   29 May 1972

Prior to this meeting the team had practised at Brands Hatch, experimenting with tyre choice and pressures and the engine had been fitted with a new cylinder head [Peter Bevan must have been busy during these championship years] and George had spent hours setting the engine up on Baldyne's rolling road.

Despite all the effort the Bevan Imp was, uncharacteristically, sat at the back of the Crystal Palace grid for the up to 1000 cc race and 1001-1300 cc race.

During the race it was a different story. Bill really pulled out all the stops and swiftly made up the deficit as he carved his way through the field and pulled away from Adams and Webb. Webb's engine unfortunately jettisoned its fanbelt and Adams, ruffled by McGovern's 'vigorous' driving, slid off into some sleepers. The end result of McGovern's labours was a class win, fastest lap, 5th overall and the Championship lead. His fastest lap was only 0.9 seconds shy of the lap record. Top ten finish number 4!

Buncombe blasts into the race lead.

Matthews, who had gambled and was running dry tyres on a wet track, lost control and hit the Armco suffering bodywork damage and was forced to retire. This dented the car and his Championship hopes somewhat. Buncombe was in great form though, and took the fastest lap and the race win.

Race 6 Brands Hatch 15 July 1972

Another mid-week practice session at Brands Hatch, and another new Peter Bevan cylinder head (power was now up to 117 bhp), ensured that the Imp was raring to go when it arrived at the circuit for the BRSCC organised Grand Prix support meeting.

This high-profile race ran at a tremendous pace, with plenty of incidents to keep the spectators on their toes. Visitor, Heikei Kemilainen, really upset the form book—by driving around the flailing opposition on his way to an excellent 1300 class win in his Escort. But, more importantly, McGovern kept out of the mêlée and calmly went on his way collecting another class win, 12th overall and fastest lap in the process. His points total was now 54: he was 9 points clear of his nearest rival, the charismatic, straight talking and supremely talented, Frank Gardner.

While the Imp's alloy engine was cooling down, Emerson Fittipaldi won the Grand Prix in a Lotus 72D.

Some corner of a foreign field

The reason for the above quotation will hopefully become clear as the following story unfolds. During the 1971 season the Bevan equipe were invited to Zandvoort to take part in the 'ADAC Dreilander Tropae'. Why? Well, it was at the behest of three German Imp racers who were using engines which George had built. They had been complaining that they could not get anywhere near the pace of the Abarths.

Blurred shot of Hans Sauer, in what is thought to be one of the 'spare' Bevan Imps.

At the time, the fastest incarnation of the 1000 cc Abarth was the TCR. This was fitted with the 8-port, twin rocker shaft 'Radiale' cylinder head and produced 116 bhp, not bad figures for a car weighing only 11.5 cwt, (some 3 cwt lighter than the Imp), especially if it was pedalled by German ace, Karl-Ludwig Weiss.

The German 'Impists' felt that Bill might be able to sort this particular Abarth out once and for all. If he did not, then, the inference being that their engines were not as powerful as they were purported to have been. One of the Imp racers was 'Bevan-ophile', Hans Sauer. He owned a nightclub in Cologne, and was instrumental in getting Bill and George over to Zandvoort.

Zandvoort   13 August 1972

Despite the pressure that was on George and Bill to win the British Championship (although there was a substantial break until the next race, which was a factor in their decision to make the trip), they took up this offer and in August the Imp was trailered to Holland. George and Bill had a point to prove.

Preparing to prove a point at Zandvoort

Although this overseas excursion barely warranted a mention in the British press, the arrival of the Bevan Imp caused tremendous interest over in Holland. Bill recalls being interviewed on radio, on TV and by magazine and newspaper reporters. In fact, the actual event—a round of The 'Deutsche Automobil Rundstrecken Pokal' (the German Saloon Car Championship and the second division of German touring car racing)—was somewhat overshadowed by what was being cited as an England v Germany confrontation (hence the Rupert Brookes's war poem quotation). The class structure for this series was really comprehensive: there were classes for 700, 850, 1000, 1150, 1300, 1600, 2000, and over 2000 cc Touring and GT cars!

Zandvoort had been chosen as neutral ground, because neither driver had competed at this circuit before. Bill managed to get in three practice sessions—breaking another doughnut in the process!

How did Bill and the Imp fare? Well, the following quote translated from a German motoring press report of the time should explain things very clearly:

> K.L.Weiss had to accept defeat. He was faced with unbeatable opposition from British champion Bill McGovern and his Bevan Imp. The Englishman was so superior, that he was about 1 second faster each lap. The winner was therefore McGovern, second Weiss.

Not only did Bill beat Weiss and his Abarth comfortably, but also through the Tarzan hairpin and complex, at the time, one of the most famous corners in racing (hence quotation) the timekeeper's stopwatch showed that the Imp had recorded the fastest times outright through that section—and this was in spite of the camshaft breaking into three pieces during the race!

Bill, always mechanically sympathetic and tuned in to the car, could feel that something was amiss with the engine. In an attempt to keep everything together, he lifted off the loud pedal a little, reducing the revs from the customary 9,400 to

7,200 rpm, whilst at the same time keeping an eye on the rear view mirror, to see how close Weiss was. Incredibly, the disintegrating camshaft kept rotating until the end of the race and enabled the Bevan Imp to record this magnificent win.

Continental drift!

It is important to appreciate that at the time Bill and the Imp were an unbeatable combination. Even someone of Weiss's calibre, would have had his work cut out trying to beat this dynamic duo at what was a 'handling' circuit. Nothing in its class, and indeed very little else could have outhandled the Bevan Imp.

Hans Sauer, who made this all happen in the first place, had an inspired day too, he came in third in class much to his amazement and great pleasure and finished right on the tail of Weiss.

Class Act

The Bevan Imp—admittedly the ultimate incarnation of a Group 2 steel-bodied Imp—beat what was a very quick Fiat Abarth, fair and square, but that said it is important to remember just how effective a racing saloon the little Abarth was.

The Abarth 850 is probably the world's first purpose-built saloon touring car and its catalogue of success on the continent is quite staggering. The genius who was responsible for the car's development and success was Carlo Abarth. He had the support of the giant Fiat Motor Company behind him and was also the undoubted master of homologation. The base vehicle for Abarth's hotshot saloon car was the diminutive Fiat 600D. Abarth succeeded in building enough cars to achieve Group 2 homologation quite early on and he even managed to get 5-speed gearboxes and rear disc brakes homologated!

By 1968 Abarth had squeezed 110 bhp from the 1000 cc engine. In 1970 the even more powerful 1000 TCR entered the fray chalking up some impressive results. Sadly, in 1971 the regulations in the ETCC changed and the smallest class division became 1300 cc. Partway through the season, Abarth & Co., feeling that it was an unequal struggle, withdrew its cars.

For the 1000 cc Abarths, competing at the very top level of saloon car racing was over, but not before they had notched up some stunning results and achievements. Over a fifteen-year period Fiat Abarths won over 7,000 races (many of them long distance endurance events), countless of these wins being attributed to the 850 and 1000 cc 'pocket rockets'.

European line-up. A gaggle of NSUs, some Abarths, a Renault Alpine and a Honda S800.
Hans Sauer, in the Bevan Imp, took the win though.

Race 7   Oulton Park   16 September 1972

After a two-month sabbatical, the competitors renewed their acquaintances at Oulton Park. The Imp had visited Brands Hatch yet again, for an extended practice session to set the car up and to run in a new engine.

Running with the front spoiler—and just look at the width of those rear tyres!

During the race the Imp of Ivor Goodwin had a most impressive outing, hanging on to the tail of the Bevan Imp for a few laps before settling for a safe second place in the class ahead of Jeremy Bean in the Mini Cooper. Melvyn Adam's race became rather fraught due to the fact that he had to take to the grass to avoid Lawrie Hickman's RS Escort. In the ensuing 'off-roading', dirt got sucked into the carburettor intakes forcing him to slow to a crawling pace to limit damage (hi-flow filters had yet to arrive on the performance scene, and race competitors usually ran the gauntlet of open intakes. Paper filters and even 'vintage' gauze trumpet covers impeded airflow and power output quite considerably).

Bill McGovern, well ahead and running in nice clean air, finished 8th overall, got another fastest lap, the customary class win, and equalled the lap record. Of much greater significance of course, was the fact that Bill McGovern's name was about to be engraved on the trophy for the third time in three years.

With five races yet to run, the team had done the unthinkable—they had completed the hat trick!

Race 8   Silverstone   24 September 1972

After a one-year hiatus the September meeting at Silverstone, the 4-hour Tourist Trophy, was reinstated. This event was Britain's contribution to the European Championship.

With the pressure off, George Bevan had entered two Imps for this meeting; Bill McGovern was trying out the spare car (but using super low-profile tyres which meant that top gear was raised to a 5.05 ratio to get maximum speed). Former Fraser Imp ace, Ray Calcutt, was going to use the Championship-winning Imp. Dieter Hendricks had brought his Hartwell-prepared version over from Germany to have a crack at the Bevan Imp.

Ray Calcutt practised and was on the reserve list. He should have got a race when Manfred Mohr non-started due to melted plugs in the Jolly Club Escort, but rather surprisingly, he was turned away, as was Andrew Webb in his Imp. The big boys, perhaps upset by the Imp's success, probably thought that one really quick Imp driver was more than enough to contend with! George was absolutely livid about the organiser's refusal to let Ray compete, which is understandable when one bears in mind that both cars had been prepared and trailered to the event. Ray had done a very good practice session and was even lined up in the pit lane before he was given the bad news.

Interestingly, in the practice session, Ray found the Bevan Imp to be superior to the Fraser Imp. It was not quite as quick, due to the extra weight it carried, but he noted that the handling was superb, the engine smooth and flexible and the top-end power slightly better. Four years of Imp development had obviously paid off.

Melvyn Adams Imp leads the Minis and another Imp.

In the first heat, Bill got the fastest lap, the class win, and 18th overall. The unfortunate Ivor Goodwin was forced to retire because of a serious lack of water in his engine, which was not exactly conducive to quick progress or engine longevity!

In the second heat, it was Bill McGovern's turn to suffer and due to a minor mechanical problem he too was forced to pit, but then rejoined and circulated slowly. He still managed to improve on the first heat placing, winning the class and crossing the finish line in 14th place. For the record, Hendrick was 36th and Adams 37th.

For this marathon event, the Bevan Imp had been fitted with the long-distance petrol tank, which held 15.3 gallons. At the finish, some 62 laps later, Doris Bevan's notes record that there was just 3 gallons of petrol left. Run flat out, as it always was, the Bevan Imp was a tad thirsty!

Race 9   Mallory Park   1 October 1972

The up-to-1000 cc and up-to-1300 cc cars made their way to Mallory for the October meeting, the penultimate event in the Championship and split into two parts.

Things did not run quite so smoothly for Bill McGovern at Mallory. It was as if the Imp was beginning to say that it had had enough. The engine began to misfire at high revs, and truly rapid progress was further impeded by four of the eight bolts shearing on one of the driveshaft couplings. Somehow, Bill managed to nurse the ailing Imp to the end of the race, finishing right on the bumper of Montague's Mini. Considering the problems he had to endure, Bill did well to coax the Imp to 6th place, fastest lap, lap record and class win.

Buncombe drove a superb race and got a very well deserved race win and fastest lap.

Race 10   Brands Hatch   22 October 1972

The final round of the RAC British Saloon Car Championship and even the dark clouds forming overhead could not dampen spirits in the Bevan camp. Ray Calcutt was at Brands Hatch in the 'spare' Bevan Imp, fingers crossed that he would get a race. Calcutt managed practice although, again, he did not get to race—George was not amused!

Bill McGovern did race though, and the Bevan Imp diced throughout, what was a wet race, with Rob Mason's Cooper 'S'—eventually managing to get past the Mini on lap 9. Rothstein threaded his Alfa Romeo past the Bevan Imp into 12th place but McGovern did not give up and was seemingly glued to the rear of the 1300 Alfa and was right on his bumper at the finish. Adam's Imp engine went sick and Webb slithered through to take second in class.

McGovern finished the season with a fine 13th overall, first in class and a fastest lap.

Table of Placings 1972 (10 rounds)				
Class Wins	Class Seconds	Lap Records	Fastest Laps	Top Ten Places
10	–	3 =1	10	2 x 8th 1 x 9th 1 x 5th (1300) 1 x 6th (1300)

We are the Champions!

Peer Recognition

George's fantastic efforts had come to the attention of the British Racing Mechanics Club. This Club is a unique organisation. It was founded in 1936 and brings together mechanics, designers, technicians and others involved in the design or preparation of cars for competitive motor sport, past, present and future.

At the end of the 1972 season the BRMC presented George with the Dunlop Mac Trophy (originally presented by Dunlop and the late Tommy Wisdom). It is awarded at the BRMC committee's discretion to a team, or an individual, for a particular or continued meritorious performance. By winning the British Saloon Car Championship on three consecutive occasions, plus all his other racing achievements, George Bevan was considered to be a worthy recipient. He was thrilled and honoured to receive this recognition for his efforts from such an esteemed organisation.

CHAPTER 7

Home Grown Hat-Trick

STOUNDING! ...Astonishing! ...Amazing!
It is very easy to run out of superlatives when describing the Bevan team's achievements. This dedicated group of people had been instrumental in winning Britain's premier Saloon Car Championship three times, with the same car and the same driver. This tremendous feat is significant enough in itself, but the fact that it was achieved by a private team makes it all the more noteworthy. It is a triumph that has never been achieved in the history of the Championship, and given the current format and requirements, it is unlikely that it ever will be repeated. So, just how did they do it?

The Car

From humble stock came a pedigree champion.

113

Once the right parts had been homologated, the Bevan Imp was quite simply head and shoulders above its opposition during the 1970 season, although that did not mean the first Championship win was easy. Forced to use a number of standard components, it was not until race 5 that a healthy degree of reliability could be guaranteed.

In 1971 the opposition woke up to the fact that this car could run away with the silverware again—if they did not do something about it. The competition was tough, and when combined with the odd error and mechanical misdemeanour you begin to appreciate just how hard the Bevan Imp had to work to capture the title. The 1971 season was an extremely hard fought one and it went all the way to the 11th round before being resolved in the Imp's favour.

For 1972, the Bevan Imp was relatively unchanged, albeit well fettled and tweaked. And, while other cars struggled to come to grips with the new regulations, the Imp—which was remarkably close to showroom specification in many ways—fairly leapt out of the starting blocks. The Bevan Imp benefited from the 1972 'J2' regulations because it was already quite corpulent. Some cars, whilst still perfectly legal, had previously been rather 'lightweight' and would suffer from the FIA-imposed 'avoirdupois'!

Over the three years, the Bevan Imp proved itself to be a real track star, with the speed of a sprinter and the stamina of a marathon runner. Not only did the car consistently destroy the opposition in its class, it pulverised a lot of the 1300s—and even 1600s. If this was not rubbing salt in the proverbial wound, the diminutive Imp was constantly finishing well inside the top ten. One can only imagine what the drivers of 1600 cc and some 2000 cc cars must have felt like when the little blue projectile passed them and then proceeded to disappear towards the horizon —usually on three, sometimes on two wheels! This was despite its relatively modest power-to-weight ratio.

Talking of weight, George should really have put the Imp on a diet, as it was consistently around a hundredweight heavier than it should have been. Removing 1 cwt is generally regarded as being equal to adding 10 bhp. It would have been very difficult to 'legally' remove weight from the Bevan Imp though but just imagine how much quicker the car could have been had it been on the class minimum.

However, George was first and foremost an engineer and was not really interested in fussing around paring the Imp's weight, and anyway the Imp is a difficult car to lighten owing to the complexity of its unitary construction. 'Stiff' cars handle better too; the suspension can do its work properly when a 'loose' and flexible shell is not corrupting responses. The Bevan Imp's handling was simply stunning, thanks to careful setting up, an extremely rigid shell, and impeccable suspension fine-tuning.

Then there is the investment, in both time and money. This car never ever wanted for anything. It was fitted with the best components that money could buy. The shock absorbers were race quality items; the wheels were the best and dressed in the stickiest and newest rubber available. However, all of these parts were 'off-the-shelf' items. The engines were lovingly assembled and regularly stripped and refreshed, as were the transaxles. If there were the merest signs of wear on any component, George would replace it. This was no lottery; nothing was ever left to chance. George was not taking part to come second!

If other competitors' pockets had been deep enough, and their commitment and dedication been equal to George's, then they too could have got their hands on the title ...perhaps.

Bill McGovern

Great friends: Bill (left) drove the car, George (right) drove the team.

Bill McGovern and the Bevan Imp were seemingly joined at the hip. Bill was a superb driver—one who could push the Bevan Imp to its absolute limits and occasionally get it to defy gravity!

He and George were great friends but their racing partnership was businesslike and utterly professional. Bill was in effect, a semi-works driver and as such was paid by George to drive the Imp. In addition he received a share of the prize money.

> I was paid quite well to drive the car. I also received forty per-cent of the prize money and bonuses. I think I was probably the best-paid driver in the Championship! George used to tell me to first dispense with all the 1-litre cars, then pick off the 1300s, a couple of 1600s and if possible a 2-litre for good measure. Most of the time I obliged!

Bill McGovern had a psychological advantage though, he had the right tool for the job, he knew that his car was the best, and he had complete and utter faith in George's handiwork.

> The car was brilliant, never once did I have to ease off to preserve the engine. George used to say that I could use it as hard as I liked!

Peter Bevan

Peter Bevan with his A40: he was good behind the wheel and with cylinder heads.

Not only was Peter a top class driver in the A40 and instrumental to the Imp's success in the club racing days, he was also an ace cylinder head man. The Bevan Imp always breathed through a Peter Bevan cylinder head. When the opposition got faster, Peter Bevan set to and extracted more torque and power. Although he retired from racing in 1968, Peter was always on hand when needed and would pitch in and help sort out any problems.

It is also important to remember that it was because Peter managed and ran the cooker business so effectively that George was able to devote so much time to the racing. Peter has no regrets though and looks back on the whole experience with much fondness.

I enjoyed racing the A40 and the Imp, it was a great time.
I am also really proud of what Dad and the team achieved with the Bevan Imp.

Peter Bevan returned to racing briefly during the 1980s and had some impressive outings in the Bevan Anglia.

Doris Bevan was great at sorting out the domestic arrangements but she was equally impressive with a stopwatch too—a real team player.

Doris Bevan provided unwavering support and was the best timekeeper that any team could ask for. Not only that, she fed and watered the team, looked after the never-ending line of visitors to 62 Leesons Hill, and she even tolerated George's use of her kitchen as a storage area (and even for the building of his engines in the early days!).

Her contribution to the success of the Bevan Imp is immeasurable. She was knowledgeable about the car, she could talk engines and transaxles—and she was brilliant at balancing the racing budget. Without doubt, the Bevan Imp would not have got where it did without her. She also enjoyed her motor racing.

> It was a great time. The house was always full of interesting people. Although I would have been happy to stop racing when Peter stopped, I was happy to support George and am very proud of what was achieved.

Sponsors & Suppliers

George brokered some good deals to get his hands on the best equipment and he had the use of some impressive facilities—but he did reciprocate by providing his sponsors with one of the fastest and best-looking mobile advertising hoardings in the UK!

The Team

George really was a genuinely nice guy, but he did not suffer fools gladly. If you were an integral part of George's team —like Keith Tilbrook, Royston Paskins, Norman Winn, Tom Simms and others were—then you were only there because you were simply the best.

Only the best ever got to work on the Bevan Imp.

George Bevan

George liked fast cars and he liked making cars go fast.

If the Bevan Imp story is about any one person, then it has to be George Bevan himself. He was, without any shadow of doubt, one of the UK's best engine and car builders (although by the beginning of the 1970s he had become totally deaf and even had to rely on Doris to tell him when to change gear in his everyday road car, because he could no longer hear the sound of the engine). George may not have driven the Imp competitively, but he certainly drove the team.

George was such a tremendous engineer and such a real gentleman, he was well respected and well liked by all who knew him. As Bill McGovern told me:

> People who knew George will always remember his happy smiling face and impish sense of humour.

Even Frank Gardner, who had cause enough to rue the Imp's success, used to pull George's leg whenever he had the opportunity. He would call the Imp everything under the sun, but in a frank and good-humoured way. Doris recalls Frank saying:

> ...that ******* car of yours runs like clockwork!

Of course, some people were suspicious over the speed and consistency of the Imp and understandably, a few questions were raised as to the legality of the car. A number of engines were certainly stripped and checked over the years, but they always proved to be 100 per cent legal. Anyone who knew George knew that he was a truly honest person. Cheating certainly was not a word that existed in the Bevan vocabulary. George was a shrewd, hardworking person, whose bedtime reading consisted of two books, race strategy and the RAC rulebook.

What he achieved with the Imp could have been replicated by any number of others, but perhaps they did not spend the pre- and post-race period carefully stripping down the engine, lapping each valve to perfection, and fine-tuning the carburation. What George was also prepared to do, and fund, was to try out new ideas and run the engines to extreme levels. When the 'test' engines exploded (and they often did!), George would have a post-mortem session where he and his mechanic(s) would scrutinise the remains to try and discover exactly what had happened. He would even devote many a lunch hour at race meetings stripping and reassembling an engine if he felt it could be made to perform even better. He spent his life in the pursuit of excellence, be it motorcycles, motorboats, motorcars or even photography.

Over the years, the path to Imp enlightenment has never been an easy one to follow, but thanks to people like George Bevan, many enthusiasts have stayed the course and found their own route to Imp fulfilment.

62 Leesons Hill as it is today with, rather appropriately, an Imp parked outside.

CHAPTER 8

Orpington and Beyond

SEMI-DETACHED success story. Not at ease with unnecessary chitchat or the post-race 'knees-ups', George positively shied away from the social side of motor racing but he could never have been described as being a recluse. 'Chez' Bevan was by no means a quiet retreat, and rarely empty (unless the Imp was racing, of course), and the Championship wins made 62 Leesons Hill even more of a honey pot for the motor racing fraternity.

Many famous (some might say infamous) team managers, mechanics and drivers paid frequent visits to the Bevan household. James Hunt had become a good friend of the family; Frank Williams visited once (he helped George get an engine for the Austin A40), and even Piers Courage and Keke Rosberg dropped in from time-to-time. Pauli Toivonen (with his son, Henri) visited the Bevan household to collect 'Bevan' engines. Top touring car driver, Steve Soper, was also a Bevan 'customer' and used a Bevan engine to good effect in his early days.

Overseas Connections
There is no doubt that George's 'passion' for motor racing impacted greatly upon everyday family life. He never had much time for holidays, although he did once nip across to Finland to see his 'export' engines in action. Occasionally foreign Imp enthusiasts would pop in to see George and sometimes they stayed too. Doris even remembers one occasion when two enthusiasts turned up unannounced and ended up staying for quite some time!

> ...there was a knock at the door and when I opened it I saw a young couple and a very, very battered Imp. The couple's names were Jamika and Jaroslav Martish and they'd driven over from Yugoslavia after having read about the Bevan Imp in the press!
>
> George completely rebuilt their Imp and was amazed at how they ever managed to get the car to us at all—it was falling apart. They stayed for a fortnight and we all got on very well, despite them speaking very little English.
>
> Just before they left, they presented me with a lovely china bowl.

At Rest and Play

George was a man who could never sit still for long; even sleep could be a problem to him, as Doris recalls:

> If there was something on his mind he would get up, get dressed and wander off to the garden shed and work throughout the night solving the problem!

Racing was George's life and the family supported him at all times, with good grace and certainly with no regrets. Despite the hectic and full racing schedule George did manage to squeeze in some time for his other interests. The almost permanently behatted and chain-smoking George—although he is not so in the three pictures in this chapter — was a keen photographer and fisherman (shark fishing being a real passion).

Over the years, he even found time to restore motor cruisers. Two of the boats were named Alison and 'J' (for Jonathan) after his grandchildren. The trouble was, he used to spend so much time making them immaculate, that he never found an opportunity to actually go and sail in them! And anyway, as soon as each boat was finished, someone would make an offer to buy one.

George relaxing with his rod and line.

Doris... look what I've gone and bought!

What Happened Next?

The team did contest the Championship in 1973, but a catalogue of incidents (mechanical and otherwise) and one serious accident effectively put paid to a fourth win. Luck certainly was not with the Bevan team in 1973.

In 1974 the Championship ran to a new format and the Imp made way for a Volkswagen Passat. The season was notable for its lack of success (mainly through homologation issues) although George and Bill did their best to make the big VW competitive.

After the VW Passat, Bill McGovern went on to race other Bevan-prepared Imps and then a Renault GT Turbo with good success. He also found time to build up a hugely successful furniture business—a business in which he is still involved with today.

Peter Bevan still lives in the Orpington area and continues to run the family cooker business. He returned briefly to racing during the late 1980s and showed that he had lost none of his talent behind the wheel.

Doris Bevan, although no longer at Leeson's Hill, still lives in Orpington. Ever since she met up with George her life has been inextricably bound up with motorbikes, cars and motorsport. She is a truly remarkable person, sharp-witted and knowledgeable. Her enthusiasm for motor racing, especially the glory years of 1970-1972, remains as strong now as it ever was.

And as for George? After the Passat venture, he stuck true to the Imp and was involved with building and running racing Imps for many years. He was also building race and road engines well into the 1990s. George remained deeply passionate about motor sport and was also on hand to help out numerous competitors and enthusiasts solve their Imp-related problems. Had he not been struck down by illness then succumbed to a subsequent infection, I am sure that George Bevan would have still been beavering away in his garden shed, tinkering with Imp racing engines, devising new ways of improving power.

George Bevan very sadly passed away on 15th March 1998. The man was legendary and thanks to his achievements, and his inspiration, his memory and legend live on.

The author took these shots inside George's 'shed' in 2002.
Although now in a bit of disarray, it still shows how George had everything he needed and to hand.

George Bevan: May 17th 1916 – March 15th 1998.

CHAPTER **9**

Fact(ory) or Fiction

THERE is a great deal of mystery, hearsay, and cloudiness surrounding the whole of the Bevan Imp story—especially its much-vaunted tie-up with the Chrysler Competition Department. This chapter tries to set the record straight and lift the veil of fog that has surrounded it.

The Bevan Imp was first and foremost, a genuinely private venture but that did not mean it was not without official backing. Chrysler were not blind to the possibility of an Imp being able to win the Championship and contrary to what some people thought—and still do think—it did actually support George Bevan in much the same way that it supported other leading privateers.

Shortly after its magnificent 1968 London to Sydney Marathon success with the Hillman Hunter, Chrysler, rather perversely, pulled the plug and officially withdrew from direct participation in competition. Much to Des O'Dell's amusement, the outside world believed this to be the end of Chrysler UK's involvement in motor sport—this could not have been further from the truth. If you had driven through Gate 5, Humber Road, Stoke, you would have found an innocuous and compact building that was home to Chrysler UK's Competition Centre. This busy department beavered away providing parts and technical assistance to anyone who used a Chrysler car in any form of competition.

The name has changed, as have the cars, but this is Humber Road, Stoke today... Rootes, Chrysler, Talbot, and Peugeot motorsports centre.

Of course the Bevan Imp fell into this category, and Chrysler helped with the provision of parts, but of greater significance, the company did provide funds to help with the running of the car. Although this fact is nigh on impossible to verify, over the three Championship years it is believed that Chrysler donated over £10,000 (possibly more), a healthy amount but far, far less than the Fraser operation was rumoured to have received, but that was as far as their support went. In fairness, the Fraser deal was brokered during the early years of the Rootes takeover, some time before the Chrysler influence truly began to make itself felt. This was a period when Imps were still held in some small esteem in various quarters (and when it was felt that they might have a future).

George's association with the factory, and its hierarchy, was very positive and it in turn was pleased with what he had achieved. Nevertheless, George's relationship with the competition department and Des O'Dell in particular, was not quite as rosy and it would be fair to say that it was not a marriage made in heaven, more a marriage of convenience. It was often fraught, especially during the early years, although there was nothing sinister about this situation; it was simply a clash of personalities. Both men were hardworking, highly capable, motivated and self-sufficient. George really was his own man and this influenced the way he did things. He never wanted to discuss the car nor the racing with Des, and he used to go straight to the directors, bypassing him, which understandably caused friction.

There are two sides to this story and it would be wise to take some time out to look at Des O'Dell's background and consider the stresses and pressure that

Des O'Dell, motorsports supremo.

he was working under. Des was chief tester at Aston Martin and then moved to their competition department where he worked on DB4 Zagatos.

He joined Rootes during 1964, and became the Chrysler Competitions manager in 1969. He was actually the first person to utilise the army testing ground at Bagshot for the development of works cars.

After withdrawing from competition, Chrysler virtually ignored the Competition Department and Des O'Dell had to work hard to justify its very existence. Chrysler, whose losses were reported to be £11 million in 1970, really did not want to know. The Department received very little in the way of direct funding and had to virtually support itself from the sales of parts and equipment via its Special Tuning arm.

In 1970 this small but pro-active department made around £65,000 from the sale of tuning goodies, of which a large percentage went to pay for staff and overheads. It is hardly surprising then, that Des was extremely cautious when it came to sharing his ever-diminishing pot of cash. Obviously, if there had been greater Competition Department involvement in the development and running of the Bevan Imp then Des might have been able to use this to his advantage. Could he have used its achievements to prise some funds out of corporate hands and into his department's coffers (for survivalist, not mercenary reasons)? Peter and Doris Bevan are of the opinion that Des wanted to to claim a greater part in the Bevan Imp's success. Unfortunately for Des, if these were his desires, they were never satiated.

George was fortunate, that through hard work, sound financial management and sponsorship, he was able to run the Imp at the highest level. He certainly was not going to let anyone other than a handpicked, non-threatening and very select few become intimate with his 'baby.'

Des O'Dell and his employees were often given short shrift by George. Despite what may have been said, written, or implied, the Chrysler Competition Department had nothing whatsoever to do with the building, development and the running of the Bevan Imp (although Des and George did confer over the specifications of certain components especially when there were breakages). There was no army of works mechanics ready to spring into action to support George, no fully equipped tow barge, no on-site catering—nil, zero, zilch. In fact, the only event where Chrysler actually 'assisted' George was the TT. He (George) hated any outside intrusion into his world and always felt that any factory involvement was, in his words:

> ...a flaming nuisance!

To be fair, the Competition Department was always on hand for all Chrysler competitors and that, of course, included George. Des O'Dell was always approachable and gave advice freely; it was just that George rarely chose to avail himself of Des's, or his department's help. Having said this, George actually spent a great deal of time at the Competition Department's stores, where Doris remembers him pestering everyone for parts and information:

> It was always busy there, and when we visited, George used to take up a lot of
> their time. I often found myself having to serve customers!

If the Imp ever had to go to the factory for publicity shots or for any technical reasons, George spent hours tinkering with the car, altering everything, so that the set-up was very different to that normally used. On one notable occasion, frustration drove Des O'Dell to comment about the way the car was presented:

> That car wouldn't be able to turn a wheel with a set-up like that!

George elected not to reply verbally—he did not have to: the expression on his face gave him away!

On another occasion, George and Doris had to visit the factory to receive a cheque for £3,500 (as part of its support in 1970). Understandably, the factory required its pound of flesh and insisted that George sign all sorts of agreements before it parted with the funds. George preferred metalwork to paperwork, and sensibly got Doris to check the documentation carefully. She discovered numerous clauses and items contained within the small print. George responded with a refusal to put his name to anything, saying:

I'm not signing that ...and I'm not signing that ...(*and so on.*)

A sort of double act ensued, with the cheque passing back and fro between George and Des. In a moment of exasperation one of Des's colleagues said:

A lot of people would like that cheque you know...

to which came the curt reply:

Well give it to them, I don't want it!

It was not that George was ungrateful—it was just that he was so fiercely independent. Eventually, a compromise was reached, and the Bevan equipe finally got their hands on the cheque.

George Bevan (back row, on extreme right) was a regular at Chrysler award functions as was Bill McGovern (front row, second from right).

Bernard Unett could really push an Imp to its limits. Here he is leading Tony Lanfranchi's Imp.

Bring your Imp up to rally performance

Performance

998cc Performance Engine (CTS 1000)
Complete 998cc engine, built to Imp Sport specification but with 998cc block and pistons. The power output of this unit is 65 bhp at 6000 rpm.

The engine comes complete with clutch, distributor, plugs, manifolds and carburettor.

If you prefer to build your own 998cc engine, we can supply a cylinder block, pistons and head gasket. To suit individual competition requirements a range of special parts is also available – such as modified cylinder heads, camshafts for road use, for rallying or for circuit racing, lightened flywheels, con rods and competition clutch.

238

Competition Exhaust System
Competition inlet/exhaust manifold for twin DCOE Weber carburettors, equally suitable for racing and rallying (CTS 1023A). Available also for rallying in a skidded form (CTS 1023B) mated up with a transverse silencer kit (CTS 1024) which gives a legal noise level.

The air cleaner (CTS 1022) is essential for any dust or dirt driving, including road use.

Suspension

Springs of varying heights and rates suitable for everything from fast road motoring to all types of competition, are available.

Shock Absorbers
CTS 1206 and 1207 are heavier duty versions of the standard fitting; CTS 1208 and 1209 are shock absorbers with competition settings for road use and club events; and CTS 1211 is for serious international competition use in the roughest conditions.

Negative Camber Kit (CTS 1201)
This kit consists of a pair of modified king pin carriers which, when fitted to a high pivot car, give $\frac{1}{2}°$ negative and, with low pivots, $2°$ negative.

Braking

This page and next: the Competition Department sold some nice Imp bits.

Competition Brake Kit (CTS 1304)
Disc brake conversions, developed for racing and road rallies such as Motoring News Championship events. Alloy calipers are included, which are not suitable for general road use and should only be used on pure competition cars.

Lined Brake Shoes (CTS 1302 & 1303)
VG95 brake linings which, allied to brake drums in a good condition, give adequate braking for all except the most rigorous conditions.

Body

Foot Brace Bar (CTS 1517)
Foot brace bar as fitted to the passenger side of 'Works' cars giving bracing for the navigator and a foot rest for the driver.

Heavy Duty Sump Guard (CTS 1601)
This is as used on 'Works' cars for rough road rallies and is capable of withstanding a tremendous amount of punishment. It covers both transaxle, sump and radiator.

Lightweight Sump Guard (CTS 1602)
This is just a skid which guards the sump and oil filter and is designed for smooth rallies and events such as Auto-cross.

Fibreglass Bonnet (CTS 1701)
Ready to accept all normal Imp fittings.

Fibreglass Boot Lid (CTS 1702)
Of Imp Sport pattern, ready to accept all normal Imp fittings.

Wheel-arch Extension Set (CTS 1704)
As homologated in Group 2. These require considerable bodywork modification to allow wider wheels to be fitted and are only the external spats to cover the wider wheels. Competition Centre can advise on how to modify the bodywork.

Instrumentation Kits
Rallye dashboard (CTS 1502) which accepts the normal switches etc. off pre-1969 cars. It also accepts the following instruments:
140 mph speedometer (CTS 1503); 200 kph speedometer (CTS 1504); 8000 rpm tachometer (CTS 1505); 2″ fuel gauge (CTS 1506);

2″ temperature gauge (CTS 1507); temperature gauge transmitter (CTS 1508).

Electrical

Competition Alternator Kit (CTS 1118)
Alternator, ammeter, control box, all the brackets and wiring etc. to fit an Imp.

Lighting
7″ Lucas Light Units of either Continental (driving) long range or fog type (CTS 1113). Lamp bar to mount four 7″ lights, (CTS 1114).

High Flange Pulley sets (CTS 1110 & 1111)
These stop the fanbelt flying off at over 7,500 rpm and alter the ratio of speeds of the water pump and either dynamo or alternator.

Engine Modifications for 875cc Engines

These are intended purely for road work. We do not recommend modifying Mk. 1 engines.

Twin 1.25 CD Kit (CTS 87501)
This is the normal Imp Sport set-up and is complete with air cleaner, and longer throttle cable.

Imp Sport Camshaft Kit (CTS 87502)
When fitting this kit to the standard Imp engine, remember that inlet valve stem oil seals should be removed.

Imp Sport Exhaust System (CTS 87503)
This is complete with all clips and brackets and represents a worthwhile improvement on standard.

Imp Sport Oil Cooler Kit (CTS 87504)
Complete with all parts necessary for the conversion, and supplied with a Competition type cooler unit.

Modified Cylinder Head Kit (CTS 87505)
This is a Sport head with 10.4:1 compression ratio, opened up and polished exhaust port and reshaped inlet port, giving a very worthwhile power increase to both sport and standard engines (further modifications are required for use with a standard engine).

The Imp was certainly not run on a shoestring, but it must be remembered that George stumped up a great deal of the funds, which were bolstered with bonus money from the high overall placings and class wins the car achieved, plus sponsorship. Chrysler's financial commitment during 1970 was alleged to have been £5,000 in total, but George often ploughed a lot of this money back into the Special Tuning Department's coffers by purchasing more parts for the car (at a discounted price admittedly).

The fact that he was never going to get his hands on George's racer eventually began to dawn on Des O'Dell, and in a surprising and rather magnanimous move, he allowed George access to all the files relating to the Works Fraser Imps. After some careful analysis of the material, George was heard to reply:

> We passed this stage years ago.

Apparently Des O'Dell was not amused! The 'frosty' relationship between George and Des eventually thawed, and in due course the two managed to develop a good 'working' relationship.

Regardless of the Bevan Imp's success, Des O'Dell obviously had not given up on the idea of running a 'factory' car and even went as far as contesting the Championship, entering saloon car ace, Bernard Unett, in an Imp. After one race, Bernard came up to Bill and George and admitted how hard he had been trying.

> I've driven my car as hard as I can, and I can't get anywhere near your time—I'm still trailing you by 1.5 seconds!

Despite this humbling experience, Des O'Dell still persevered but to little avail. Bill was quite bemused by their attitude.

> It seemed a silly idea to enter Bernard in the same class as us, if they wanted an Imp to win the Championship. However the situation was resolved when we soundly beat him at Oulton Park, outqualifying him by 1.6 seconds. This was in spite of Bernard being one of the best drivers in the country, but the Bevan Imp was so much better than the rest.

Perhaps it was because of this very public nose blooding, that Des O'Dell once resorted to try and 'downgrade' the Bevan Imp's success? In one interview, he freely admitted that, in his opinion, the Bevan Imp won the Championship due to luck because Ford had unaccountably left the 1000 cc class wide open. This kind of statement smacked of sour grapes—it was also wide of the mark. The truth of the matter was that the highly stressed 1000 cc Ford engine did not seem to work well enough for long enough. The Mini Coopers were simply not powerful enough, and even the 1300 Escorts had difficulty in beating the Bevan Imp. Of the other Imps, even those prepared by legendary Imp specialist, Team Hartwell, could not get near to the pace of the Bevan Imp.

Des was an Imp enthusiast though, and even managed on one occasion to get the special wet-liner 998 engines built on the normal production line—until someone asked for a power graph for a 998 cc engine and the plot was found out!

George Bevan.

The winning team.

The Imp.
Prepared by George Bevan.
Driven by Bill McGovern.
All winners for the last three years in the British Saloon Car Championships.
You can also be in the winning team with Chrysler. Chrysler, who make cars for the sports enthusiast.
There's the complete range of five Hillman Imps. The Avenger Tiger II.
And option packs to turn an Avenger into a Tiger.
Don't be left standing. Come on in to your nearest Chrysler dealer and get the car you want. With the options you want.

HILLMAN

CHRYSLER
UNITED KINGDOM

Chrysler make the cars you want.

CHRYSLER
SUNBEAM
HUMBER
SIMCA

Too little, too late?

Des even wanted to enter an Imp in the London to Sydney Marathon. It would not have lasted the course, but he felt that it could have held the lead for a time, and got some excellent publicity.

Missed Opportunity

One would naturally think that Chrysler would have leapt at the chance to capitalise on the Bevan Imp's success, especially bearing in mind that the Imp was not the best of sellers, not to mention its less than robust public image.

Three decades on, memories are understandably a little dimmed, but the family feels aggrieved that Chrysler's publicity machine did little to enlighten the general public as to enormity of the Bevan Imp's success. It was not entirely the factory's fault though, when it came to publicity and in any dealings with the factory, George—as discovered—could be a tricky customer.

In terms of its promotion of the Bevan Imp Chrysler failed dismally. In 1970, the car did feature on the Chrysler UK stand at the Earls Court Motor Show and in the occasional advert, but bearing in mind the incredible success the car would go on to achieve over a three-year period, there was not the deluge of promotion you would have expected.

George harboured the hope that Chrysler would produce a sporty roadgoing version of the Bevan Imp. He was not averse to letting the company use the 'Bevan' moniker in the same way that Fiat and BMC used the Abarth and Cooper names. However, George Bevan was an individual, not a tuning establishment in the way that Abarth and Cooper were. There was no factory, no production facility; and it simply was not viable nor practical even to consider the possibility of a highly stressed race-inspired Imp variant hitting the showroom without such a life support system.

Imp enthusiasts wanting a quicker production Imp had to content themselves with the Imp Sport and Stiletto variants. Nice cars but 'warmed-up' rather than race-tuned. If you wanted more urge, then the competition department could help, as it had a huge range of well-developed parts and specialist services available. Of course, there were other options available: you could also head in the direction of Chrysler Competition Centre in Coventry, Ray Payne at Team Hartwell in Bournemouth, Andy Chesman at Greetham Engineering in Coventry or Ian Carter in Bedford.

Chrysler handouts aside, the 1970, 1971 & 1972 Championship winners had basically and quite simply, done it themselves. In the Bevan household, racing dominated. George Bevan and Bill McGovern had taken on the very best the UK and Europe had to offer and simply beaten them— fair and square!

Number 1 says it all.

CHAPTER **10**

Ice Racers

ECAUSE of the success of the Bevan Imp, George Bevan became well known and widely respected in the UK. Whilst this chapter is slightly out of context regards the British Saloon Car Championship, the intention is to illustrate how the Bevan influence extended quite a way beyond our shores. In Finland, for example, amongst the Imp fraternity, George's reputation and status was, and still is, second to none.

Finland boasts an incredible 190,000 lakes and around one quarter of the country's total area lies within the Arctic Circle. So what better winter pastime than ice racing on the frozen lakes and what better vehicle to do it with than a Bevan-engined Imp on skinny studded tyres?

From the late 1960s through until the mid-1990s, Imps virtually cleaned up in ice racing. Even today, Imps continue to do well and there is something of resurgence in Imp interest in Finland. A number of historic rally and race Imps have been, or are in the process of being, rebuilt. Spectators on historic events are once again becoming accustomed to the sight and sound of well-driven and immaculately prepared Imps.

Over the years, a number of drivers had good cause to thank George Bevan for providing such robust and powerful engines, the most famous was Pauli Toivonen and overall, the most successful was probably Juhani Kynsilehto. It was not just the drivers that came under the Bevan spell, the mechanics often found themselves being caught up in the magic too.

The following accounts are from Juhani Kynsilehto and Timo Saaristo and are reproduced verbatim as the author received them, because their narratives were felt to be so much better in their unedited state.

Juhani Kynsilehto

Juhani—or 'Jussi', as he is known—was the First Finn to drive a rallycross Imp in a factory team and had been the Finnish Motocross Champion. In the late 1960s and early 1970s, Kynsilehto was sales manager at the Wihuri concern, the importer of Imps in Finland (managed by Pauli Toivonen). A keen and able competitor with motorcycles, rally and race cars he also had the privilege to drive some of the Imp rallycross-specials for Chrysler UK in England.

In addition to the ice racing, Jussi was a professional works rally driver—driving for such teams as Ford, Opel, Fiat and Polski-Fiat. One of his claims to fame is the longest-ever recorded yump, at 72 metres! In the 1970s one of Jussi's main co-drivers was Martin Holmes of esteemed publication *Pirelli World Rallying*.

Jussi retired from rallying in 1984.

From Jussi Kynsilehto...

The years 1971, -72, -73, -74, and 1975 have remained indelibly in my mind as one of the brightest and most glorious motor sport years I ever had, as I had just before year 1970 moved from Moto-Cross to track racing.

I met George Bevan for the first time in the spring of 1970 while visiting him in England, Kent Orpington. This was the time we agreed with George of the first engine he would be supplying for me, which indeed lead immediately to Finnish Championship silver position and was followed by two Finnish and Swedish Championship victories. In the English Championships I was never able to beat George Bevan's night-blue devil, which was driven by George's very talented driver Bill McGovern. At my best I was, almost every single time, right behind him in the British Championship Racing as a good number two.

The co-operation with George was incredibly beautiful. During my several racing trips to England, Doris and George Bevan's home in Orpington was like a second home to me.

Not only that, George Bevan was an excellent builder of cars and especially an insuperable tuner of Imp engines, as a person, like his always kind wife Doris, were the most significant and highly appreciated motor sports friends I had during the whole 22 years career in motor sports. During this time I had met, while competing in 16 different European countries, several of the influential persons in the field and persons with whom I have stayed lifetime friends, in the end amongst these friends, whose value can not be measured in money, George Bevan is the number one.

George did not actually build me the whole racing car, but he supplied to all the Imps that I drove to victory, the engines, as well as Jack Knight's special gears with sintered clutches. In the building of the suspension to the cars, George Bevan supplied us vital components such as special shock absorbers, stabilizators, special brake plates etc.

The best-finished race Imp I bought from Warwick near Birmingham, which also carried in its tailbox the legendary register number REG-3. The fact was that REG-3 was one of the best Imp's I ever had and naturally George Bevan supplied the engine and gearbox for this car.

After I sold REG-3, the following Race Imps were build in Finland, according to the blue devil of George Bevan and with his instructions. The cars were later built by Paavo Anttila, who also had accomplished himself as a winner of Finnish Icetrack Championships with Bevan engines. Paavo was trained by George in Orpington and followed by this he got himself an honorary name of 'Bevan of Pulkkila'! Another one of my mechanics was Veikko Lepistö who was also trained by George in Orpington, and was with Paavo Anttila one of the best Imp mechanics on the racetracks of Scandinavia. Also third one of my mechanics, Risto Heikkinen, with whom during the Rally Cross days I toured the European Championships, was trained by George Bevan.

Austria 1973, a victorious Jussi sits on the bonnet of his European Championship-winning Imp.
(opposite page: REG 3 in action at Thruxton).

Ice racing in Swedish Championships 1974.

Ice racing Imp in tarmac trim.

As the most significant accomplishments during my Hillman Imp competing years I keep the two Finnish Championship victories, two of the Swedish Championship victories, (there was within two years, eight events hard as stone, up-to-1300cc, 25 driver finals driven) in which I got seven victories and one second place. The memorable races and great results achieved were in

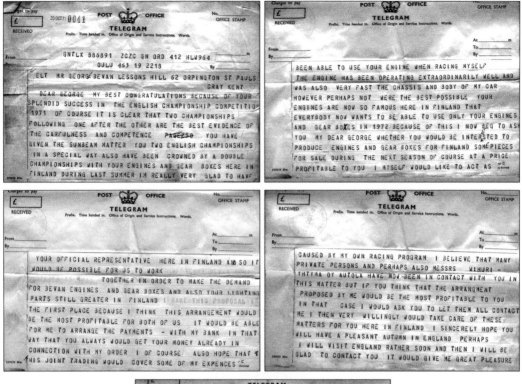

Telegrams from Jussi to George in October 1971

Thruxton, Oulton Park, Silverstone, Branch Hatch, England, Melk in Austria, Knutstorp in Sweden and above all Pavia, Italy.

These are the most memorable races I drove Imp and George Bevan's engines in. Although, we are now living the year 2004 and 4-wheel drive cars have reached the European Championships of rally cross, with engine powers three times the ones in Imp, I think that the Pavia, Italy track record is still in our name. The car was of course with George Bevan engine.

I remember now and always will as one of the most heartbroken days of my life, one Friday morning couple of years ago as I opened my mail at the office, the letter revealed a letter send by Doris Bevan. There was an invitation for

Saturday memorial ceremony of our beloved and highly appreciated George Bevan. It was a moment that seized my blood and almost stopped my heart from beating. Because of the short notice, I had no possibility to participate in the memorial, but we had an opportunity to have our daughter Anne-Marie, who lives in England, to commiserate in the memorial with blue and white (The National colours of Finland) flowers, in the ribbon there were the names of all the George's Finnish friends and mechanics, Paavo's, Veikko's, Riku's and mine.

Sincerely,

Jussi (John - the name George used to call me by) Kynsilehto

The Flying Finn Driver of George Bevan

CEO Oy In-Oilers & Engineering Ltd., Finland.

Positive attitude... Ukko Kervinen, Finnish Imp pioneer, leads Pedro Rodriguez's Fiat Abarth.

Some Finnish Imp History from Jussi Kynsilehto

Ukko Kervinen, Mr. Imp of Finland, is one of the most famous Hillman Imp drivers and a specialist of Imp engines. He was also the dealer of Hillman Imp for Northern Finland and his sales volume was the biggest in the Finnish Imp market.

One of his main mechanics was Mr. Veikko Lepistö, who he wanted to be trained by Mr. George Bevan in England. Later, Mr. Veikko Lepistö started to work as a head mechanic for Jussi Kynsilehto and he was with Mr. Paavo Anttila, the very elite of Bevan engine specialists in Finland.

We can justifiably state that Ukko Kervinen is the starter of the whole Hillman Imp competition racing and driver with a burning soul as well as a top constructor of Imps. Ukko Kervinen was seen in the starting line in every large scale Rallies of Finland, such as Thousand Lakes Rally, Hakkapeliitta Rally, Pohjola Rally, Arctic Rally and in countless other ice races in different parts of Finland.

In the pit stops of Keimola and Ahvenisto he was a legend as a definition. The spring race in the track of Artukainen was the opening race of summer season for Ukko Kervinen – and he raced naturally with nothing but the Hillman Imp!

Ukko Kervinen was the very first one in Finland to start racing with the Hillman Imp – later came Mr. Pauli Toivonen, the European Champion of Rally, Jussi Kynsilehto, multiple Champion of Finland and countless other top drivers. This group of drivers formed the famous team of Härmän Häjyt. Along with Mr. Toivonen and Kynsilehto, the drivers to win with the Bevan engine were Mr. Hannu Pohjola from Varkaus and the legendary Bevan of Pulkkila, Mr. Paavo Anttila.

Update

Hannus Pohjola bought REG 3 from Juhani Kynsilehto and raced it with great success. Currently, his son, Jari, is restoring this Imp to its former glory.

Ice dancing.

Pauli Toivonen

Pauli was 1968 European Rally Champion, the driver of the 'winning' Citroën on the 1966 Monte Carlo rally, (the event which was notable for the Mini headlight debacle).

Pauli Toivonen used an Imp to become Finnish Ice Racing Champion in 1970. He also became a close friend of the Bevan family. He is also father to Harri and Henri Toivonen (Henry was tragically killed on the 1986 Tour de Corse). Timo Saaristo was the mechanic charged with the responsibility of looking after the car.

Getting to grips with the competition.

From Timo Saaristo…

My trip started from Helsinki, where local Finnish Chrysler imported was located. My boss Pauli Toivonen send me to take his racing Imp first to the factory competition centre in Coventry in order to make some body and suspension modifications for the car with the factory mechanics. I was hosted by Des O'Dell and Andy Dawson who worked there at that time.

After this work I went to meet George Bevan, Toivonen had ordered a new racing engine from him. I met George in Silverstone circuit where were British racing car races. Bevan Imp was taking part driven by Bill McGovern. George had arranged a paddock ticket for me and I found him and his team in their caravan. I was so welcomed at the first minute by him and his wife Doris.

Soon the race started and we went to the pits, unfortunately Bill came to the pits after few laps, oil cooler had started to leak and the race was over for him. So we went back to the caravan and watched the rest of the race at TV.

In the evening we drove his home near by London, I left the racing car in his garage and George took me to the hotel, which he had booked for me. When we came to the hotel we had difficulties to find any personnel in there, at last owner came. George asked to see the room, we went there, and George said, 'Timo this is not good, you come to stay in my house.' And we drove back and I lived with their fantastic hospitality my four-day stay.

Monday morning we started to build up the engine with his mechanic (I can't remember the name) In the evening we sat in his living room and talked about the Imps and the racing, and every evening few local 'Imp men' came with a cylinder head or cam shaft to visit him. George welcomed always all and took old newspapers to cover the coffee table so we could examine the parts and have long nice discussions about the subject. Mrs Bevan was serving coffee and tee with cookies and did not mind that we had engine parts on her coffee table.

After few days we get the engine ready and fitted it to the car, and that sounded very nice. So my trip in England was finish and I started to get back to Finland. And I still remember the great hospitality which George and his nice wife gave me at that visit.

Thank You George.

* * *

CHAPTER **11**

Personality Profiles

OTOR RACING is a tremendous sport—man and machine in perfect harmony—most of the time anyway! Nevertheless, for a pastime /occupation that is so machine-orientated, the cars often play second fiddle to their talented and oft-charismatic drivers.

When first researching the material for this book, I too was guilty of just looking at results achieved by the cars, especially the Bevan Imp. It did not take long for the realisation to dawn that this was not just about the cars or a car—no matter how successful it was—it was also about the people involved. From thereon the focus of my attention shifted as I delved deeper into the lives of those personally involved—the drivers, the mechanics, and the families.

It really was a journey of discovery and my horizons began to broaden. I soon began to really think about the other drivers who competed at the time and who had been part of the Bevan Imp era—even fallen under its spell, perhaps? To get a far more rounded story I needed to track down, then interview a selection of the personalities who were racing during the glorious Bevan Imp period. Then there was the historical perspective with Jack Sears—as the first British Saloon Car Champion, he just had to be included. He was a fantastic racing driver and his contribution to the sport is enormous. Then there was Ray Calcutt's exploits with the Fraser Imps—the stuff of legend—and the Fraser Team's achievements led directly to George Bevan choosing an Imp over the Anglia. It is fair to say that without Alan Fraser's efforts there probably would not have been a Bevan Imp.

With so many personalities to choose from the task of selecting the 'other' drivers was not an easy one. In the end, and after much thought, I made the selection of the following group. I thoroughly enjoyed interviewing all of the drivers and became captivated by what they had achieved and what they had to tell. I hope that you will enjoy reading their profiles as much as I enjoyed meeting and talking with them.

Jack Sears — The First British Saloon Car Champion

Shortly after the conclusion of the Second World War, Britain, once again, began to reverberate to the sound of highly-tuned racing engines. The now redundant airfields were proving to be ideal locations for motorsport. Brooklands, as a racing venue was sadly no more, but Goodwood circuit opened its doors in 1947. In 1948, Silverstone ran its very first Grand Prix the same year that a young man by the name of Jack Sears began his racing career.

Jack Sears — Gentleman Racer

Like father, like son—or so the saying goes—and Jack Sears was certainly influenced and encouraged by his father. Stanley Sears was a well-respected and successful race and rally driver during the inter-war years and it was he who provided Jack with his first car, a brand new Morgan 4/4. And, it was with his father's blessing and approval that Jack joined the 'Brighton and Hove Motor Club' using the 4/4 to contest a number of its events. The Malvern machine proved reasonably effective but the inevitable desire to go that bit faster led to the acquisition of a quicker car, one that sported that famous octagonal badge:

> In 1948, I competed in speed trials, rallies and autotests, using the Morgan. It was a good car, but not quite quick enough, so in 1949 I swapped the Morgan for a MG TC. I also did some vintage speed events in my father's 1914 TT Sunbeam.

The following year continued in much the same vein but in 1950 Jack, who had proved himself to be a very talented driver, switched his attention to circuit racing.

> My first race was at Goodwood in the MG, then I did a vintage race meeting at Silverstone using the Sunbeam.

In addition to the MG and the Sunbeam, over the next five years, he raced a Cooper MG, Jaguar XK 120 Roadster, XK 120 FHC and a Lister-Bristol. Heady stuff indeed, but the young charger was more than equal to the challenges these cars dished out.

The 1950s racing scene was somewhat elitist, dominated as it was by single-seaters and sports cars, but like many others, Jack could not fail to notice the slow but steady ascendancy of saloon car racing. Thanks to the pioneering efforts of the British Racing Drivers' Club and the *Daily Express*, who helped with funding at Silverstone, this emergent category was becoming hugely popular. Jack was captivated by the spectacle these cars provided, and wanted in on the action. Unfortunately, without a suitable car at his disposal and under contract to BMC as a works rally driver for 1956, some twelve months would elapse before he could fulfil this desire.

BMC, although heavily involved with the Healey rally programme, had dabbled with saloon car racing as well. In a forward-thinking move, the company 'lent' Jack an A105 in 1957, which he raced with great success. When BMC got wind that there was going to be a 'proper' Saloon Car Championship for 1958 it acted. The A105 had proved itself swift enough and Jack was the obvious choice as its driver, so in 1958 he became a 'Works-supported privateer'.

The term 'Works support' conjures up an image of a team of mechanics and a van full of spares pandering to his every whim. The reality however, could not be further from the truth—Jack had to buy and run his own car (the A105 he had used in 1957) and as driver/entrant the onus of responsibility for the racing programme lay firmly at his own feet. Not that this proved too much of a problem though:

> It was so simple back then. Before each race, all I did was check oil and water levels and put some extra air in the tyres! If anything major needed doing to the car, I'd have to take it to the competition department at Abingdon. They'd provide a loan car and I'd drive back home. When the work was done I have to repeat the process. Of course, we drove our cars to events in those days too.

Jack clocked up plenty of miles but, by and large, the roads were very quiet and these journeys provided opportunities to hone driving skills and explore the big Austin's outer limits!

Despite the friendly atmosphere that pervaded the paddock, the racing was deadly serious. Jack remembers having some terrific dices as he raced through to head the 'class of 58'.

> Harold Grace put up some good fights in his Riley Pathfinder and I had some great battles with Jeff Uren. He was a superb driver—the only Zephyr driver ever to beat me. Tommy Sopwith and I were great friends off-track but tremendous rivals on it.

The A105 remained Jack's mainstay throughout 1959 although he also raced Tommy Sopwith's Jaguar 3.4 (Sopwith had retired at the end of 1958) and an Austin-Healey. The Healey did, in fact, start the season as a 100/6, only to end up as a 3000—having been re-badged and 'upgraded' by the factory in line with the new production model.

Jack may not have managed to repeat his Championship win, but he was, nevertheless, going to the top—his prowess behind the wheel had caught the attention of team managers and he spent the next two years racing the cream of sporting machinery. How about this for an 'A' list of desirable cars? Jaguar 3.8 Mark 2, Aston Martin DB4 GT, Formula 2 Cooper, Jaguar E-types, Ferrari 250 SWB, 250 GTO and 330 LMB and, of course, the thundering Galaxie and a variety of Cortinas (GT and Lotus).

> I did the début race for the Cortina GT where I won the class. This was the first win for a Cortina—anywhere in the world.

Each of these cars provided many memorable moments and podium places, but in Jack's opinion there is one amongst them with real star quality.

> The Ferrari 250 is the most perfect car I have ever raced and has the most wonderful attributes. As well as its amazing power and perfect balance, it is also incredibly reliable. It is, without doubt, the most fantastic car.

1963 was a vintage year for Jack. Sharing a Ferrari 330 LWB with Michael Salmon he finished a highly creditable 5th at Le Mans. Back on home soil and racing for the Willment Team, stints behind the wheel of a Cortina GT, Lotus Cortina and Galaxie proved highly successful and he lifted the British Saloon Car title once more.

The landing carrier-sized Galaxie was like a racing dinghy in Jack's capable hands.

1964 would prove to be equally hectic. Willment wanted him to race its Cobra in the Goodwood TT. But, Cobra development was in its infancy and while Jack was deliberating the prospect of driving the yet-to-be-sorted and rather unruly Cobra, John Coombs approached him with a very tempting offer.

> I was in a very fortunate position at this time because I had established myself as a quick driver. John Coombs wanted me to drive his 'lightweight' E-type Jaguar in the TT. Willment were very understanding when I told them about this offer. They acknowledged that the Cobra needed some more work so they allowed me to race the Jaguar.

Work continued apace on the Cobra(s) and Jack drove a succession of these cars during the 1964 season. There was the Willment Cobra Roadster, then the Willment Cobra Coupé a fabulous looking and very successful car constructed with the blessing of Carroll Shelby himself. Jack also raced AC Car Company's own Cobra, the AC Cobra Coupé. By the end of the season he had become well used to the brutish but endearing characteristics that these cars exhibit.

1965 was the Jim Clark year, and Jack was teamed up with the Formula One ace and drove a factory Lotus Cortina in the British Saloon Car Championship. Jack was also contracted to Colin Chapman and in between his duties as test driver he also raced a Lotus 30. When not racing in the UK, Jack could be found overseas competing in the World GT Championship in a Shelby Daytona Cobra coupé. 1965 was also notable in that it was also the year that he retired—and the year that he very nearly lost his life.

Having completed the season Jack did some testing with a Lotus 40.

> This was the car that Jim Clark was due to race in California. I'd done some testing at Snetterton and Colin Chapman wanted me to do some laps at Silverstone. I went to Silverstone and ran it through the morning session with no problems. After lunch we tried different types of tyres and I was unlucky enough to go off at Abbey Curve.

The Lotus 40 inexplicably left the track and, in the ensuing and quite horrific crash, Jack's arm flew up and became trapped between the rollover hoop and the road. When he was pulled free from the wreckage it was discovered that his arm was broken and scalded (when the header tank split), his hand had been virtually severed and his neck, to all intents and purposes, had been broken! Jack was rushed to hospital where Ken McKee (the pioneer of the artificial hip) managed to save his hand and repair the damage using a combination of bone grafts, skin grafts and steel plates. The scald damage was also repaired using skin grafts. Although the arm and hand had been saved, Jack found that he had very little mobility and none of his fingers would move. With months of hard and determined work on Jack's part and the skills of his physiotherapist most, but not all, of the movement returned. Thankfully, the neck injury healed itself naturally.

1966 was the 'lost' year because it was effectively a period of recuperation and regeneration. His fitness returned and although he would never be able to swing a golf club any more, driving and game shooting would not pose a problem for him. At the end of 1966 Jack reflected on what had gone before and what the future held for him.

> My wife had been most patient with my racing, my son was 11 and my daughter had not long been born. Ken McKee said that if I got another bang on my head I might not be so lucky next time. So, I stopped racing.

Jack did, however, make several guest appearances including one in the Mexico Challenge at Brands Hatch—which he won! Gerry Marshall asked him to race his Dolomite Sprint at Mallory Park in 1978 where he finished second in class and fourth overall. Jack's life has been, and always will be, inextricably bound up with motor sport. He still owns the 1963 Championship-winning Galaxie and a facsimile of his first racing MG TC. His son David, who now runs a Formula Three team, raced for fifteen years, getting a 3rd place at Le Mans with Anthony Reid and Tiff Needell.

...Like father, like son.

Frank Gardner — The Impressive all-rounder

Having been a boxing, swimming, and rowing champion, not to mention a pretty swift speedway rider, Frank Gardner's sporting credentials are a little bit more than impressive, but it is his career as a racing driver for which he is best known.

Not only was he the first racing driver in the world to chalk up one-hundred race wins, but he has also competed in well over four-hundred races. He was also a work's driver for Ford, Porsche, General Motors, Brabham, and Lola—as well as having driven for a large number of private teams. Twice British Champion Racing Driver, European Formula 5000 and European Formula 2 Champion, Frank was seemingly able to drive competitively and successfully in any type of car.

Frank Gardner puts an Alan Mann Racing Escort through its paces.

Frank Gardner poses by one of the many race cars he drove: here it is a Ford GT40.

1967 and Frank is getting to grips with the Falcon.

Frank Gardner is widely considered to have been the toughest-ever saloon car racer and his skill and commitment behind the wheel of a host of different tin-tops netted him not only the European Touring Car Championship, but the European Saloon Car title and he was also British Saloon Car Champion on three occasions.

Five years on in April 1972 and Frank wrestles the powerful Camero at Thruxton.

It was during his British Saloon Car Championship period, that he met and became friends with George Bevan and Bill McGovern.

When asked for his thoughts about George, Bill, and the Bevan Imp, Frank recalls it all so very well:

> Saloon cars were the chosen paths for a lot of people. It was a kind of proving ground and the British Saloon Car Championship was a series of races where people were well observed. George Bevan was a clever bloke—he could rub two boy scouts together and make a fire! He set about winning the Championship professionally. The Bevan Imp was immaculate, and prepared like a Swiss watch and driven in a far superior way to anything else in its class. George used to make Chinese cookers and I used to joke that the Bevan Imp went so well, for lap after lap, it could 'Wok around the clock!'
>
> Bill drove the car surprisingly well. Not only did he have a high degree of skill, he also had the ability to finish. Bill was able to cope with the wide variety of cars that were on the track at the same time. He was courteous and gave me and other drivers in the powerful Camaros and Mustangs, plenty of room.
>
> I don't think he or the car was marketed well enough, but back then, everything wasn't as commercial as it is now and the opportunities were limited.
>
> The whole team were such nice people, especially George.

After retiring from racing in 1977, Frank remained in motor sport, but on the managerial side. He is one of the world's foremost authorities on driving and driving safety. Today, Frank is managing director of the Holden Performance Driving Centre on Australia's Gold Coast.

Frank Gardner racing the Alan Mann Racing Ford P38.

Ray Calcutt — Inspiration

A career as a traffic officer with the Kent Police paid the bills but Ray Calcutt's heart was set on becoming a racing driver. Thanks to his dogged persistence and a helping hand from Alan Fraser, Ray was able to make the transition from patrol car to racing car. One of the sports gentlemen drivers, he was polite and quiet off the track, but a true racer on it.

A passionate motor racing enthusiast, Ray took every opportunity to visit Alan Fraser's Mountains Garage at Hildenborough in Kent, ostensibly to visit a friend who worked there, but there was a much more serious motive behind his regular visits. Ray picks up the story:

> I used to pester Alan about how I could get started in motorsport and my perseverance eventually paid off. One afternoon Alan asked me what I was doing the next day as he was trying out a driver in a Sunbeam Rapier at Brands Hatch. If I turned up, there could be a chance that I would get a drive. If I was available he would take a second Rapier.

Ray's first proper racing car—the ex-works Alpine.
(in the background can be seen some of the garages at Fraser's Hildenborough headquarters).

155

Ray did turn up. He was given the opportunity to get some laps in and set about extracting the most he could from the Rapier—without any heroics! He went well. Well enough to convince Alan Fraser of his potential as a racing driver. The following year Ray had many successful outings in the ex-works Fraser Le Mans Sunbeam Tiger, and by the end of the 1964 season he had done enough to get his full racing licence. Just as he was pondering what 1965 would hold for him, Alan Fraser approached him with a proposition, one that did not immediately thrill Ray. As Ray explains:

> Alan had been racing and rallying Rootes products for 13 years and he felt that it was now time to turn his attention to the new Imp and would I be interested in driving one? I didn't wish to appear ungrateful, but to be honest what I'd seen and heard about the Imp hadn't filled me with confidence!

Ray may not have been keen, but Alan Fraser's engineers, John Griffiths and Brian Pritchard-Lovell, most certainly were. They were masterminding the Imp's racing development programme and positively radiated enthusiasm for Rootes' new baby. They sat Ray down and swiftly enlightened him as to why they were so fanatical about this project. By the end of their discussions Ray was a convert—almost! He had to admit that on paper the Imp looked good. It was rear-wheel-drive, had near perfect weight distribution and the added advantage of a Coventry-Climax-based engine. Ray still needed to be convinced about how it would perform on the track, so Alan entered Ray and the Fraser Imp at a Sunbeam Talbot Owners' Club sprint. Although Imp tuning was in its infancy this, the earliest incarnation of a Fraser Imp was still pretty special.

Ray and the Fraser Imp 'clicked':

> I couldn't believe how well the Imp went and how beautifully balanced it felt. I not only managed to get first in class but also fastest time of the day!

If Ray was pleased with this result, Alan Fraser was almost ecstatic! He knew the Imp had potential, but harboured concerns about its race reliability. These concerns were well founded. After all, Rootes garages were stuffed full of Imps having their gaskets and water pumps changed not to mention a catalogue of other mechanical maladies attended too. And, we have to bear in mind that Alan Fraser was a man used to the long-legged durability of Sunbeam Alpines and Tigers. Still, a class win and FTD against much more powerful opposition augured well and effectively kick-started the next stage of the Fraser Imp development programme.

Alan Fraser ran Ray in 1965 and yes, reliability issues did come to the fore, but little-by-little the problems were overcome—as Ray recalls:

> We'd lead a race for 8 laps then the head gasket would let go, or the fanbelt would jump off the pulleys. But, as the year progressed, the reliability improved greatly and we started to move up the field.

At the end of the year, Ray and the Fraser Imp had over 30 awards to their credit and the future looked good. Good enough in fact for Rootes to make Fraser the official works-backed team. This was a shrewd move, as in 1966 the 'works' Fraser Imps started to rack up win after win.

Cover picture from a Fraser Imp brochure (Ray Calcutt driving).

On the circuits things were running pretty smoothly for Ray was finding that his life had become something of a juggling act and he had begun to drop the odd ball. He freely admits:

> Because of all my racing commitments I was getting back late, then going on night duty. My racing commitments were definitely having an adverse effect on my career. Occasionally my crew member would spot something that should be investigated, but in my mind, I was still driving around Snetterton or Brands.

He also took quite a lot of risks in the pursuit of his racing. If there were a race or practice at Brands Hatch, Ray would park his police patrol car close to the circuit and spectate. One day, however, he was truly caught out:

> The radio crackled into life and I was asked for a location check. To cover myself I made up a location, which was some distance away. When I got into the station later that day, the inspector informed me that I couldn't have been where said I was because he could hear the sound of racing cars in the background!

Ray became increasingly concerned that he was not fulfilling his role as a police officer, so it came as a relief when Alan Fraser offered him a permanent job.

Although his position was primarily a driving one, he also undertook a lot of development and promotional work too, but his time at Mountains Garage was all too short-lived. Just when it seemed as if everything was going well for Alan Fraser Engineering, Rootes (now owned by Chrysler) had a change of heart and in 1968 pulled the plug on all active participation in motorsport. For Alan Fraser, who had put his heart and soul into the Imps, not too mention in a huge amount of his own money and time, this proved too much to bear. He quickly became disheartened and within a few years he had retired from the UK motor racing scene and moved to Tenerife. When the Fraser operation was wound up, Ray had the opportunity to acquire one of the Fraser Imps (complete with gearbox, but minus engine), which he then put into storage. Ray, quite understandably, is eternally grateful for the help he received from Alan Fraser.

> I was an unknown and am indebted for the help I got from Alan and without him I would never have become a racing driver.

With the Fraser era over Ray began work locally in retail car sales and switched to racing the Lenham GT P80. The combination of this fantastic car, fitted with a mildly tuned 1558 cc Lotus twin-cam engine, plus Ray, proved to be highly effective. Ray won the 1969 *Motoring News* GT Championship in style, taking many wins and class records along the way—as he recalls:

> It was a brilliant time. We were winning everywhere. It even ran out of revs at Thruxton but still came in first!

In addition to racing the Lenham GT, Ray also raced a Brabham F3 and had a number of very successful outings.

The stunningly beautiful Lenham G.T.

Ray also raced Alan Fraser's F5000 Lola in 1970 and in his spare time he began to resurrect the Fraser Imp although he did not really have enough funds to compete, let alone buy the requisite full-race engine. Happily for Ray, Imp supremo and all-round nice guy, George Bevan had learnt of his plight and offered support and even loaned him an engine. Ray also got assistance from his friend Graham Coombe (nicknamed 'Grimble') who helped prepare the car.

With the engine sorted, all that Ray needed was a suitable tow car and he found one—dumped, as it happened, in a barn behind Mountains Garage. The car, a Humber Super Snipe Estate, was duly fettled and then pressed into service as a tow car, a duty that it performed admirably.

Although George Bevan had been happy to loan Ray an engine, one of his stipulations was that after every third race the engine had to be brought back to him to be checked over. George had a reputation to maintain and this was a condition that Ray was more than happy to comply with.

Graham and I used to remove the engine, put it in the back of the Super Snipe and take it up to George's house in Orpington. He would then check it over, fit new cam followers or whatever and put it back together.

Crystal Palace, September 1972. Ray at full pelt and on his way to the lap record and class win.

The Bevan engine proved to be an inspiration and this diminutive powerhouse pushed Ray all the way to the 1971 *Practical Motorist* Saloon Car Championship title and the *Kent Messenger* series also in 1971. He was fortunate in securing sponsorship from *Kent Messenger* and *Speed International* at Brands Hatch, as he was also racing a McLaren M18 F5000 as well.

By the mid-1970s the Calcutt trophy cabinet was full of assorted plaques, plates and cups, but for a variety of reasons Ray's racing career was put on hold. This situation persisted until the beginning of 1984 and things gathered speed again when he entered his 'Japanese' period.

Ray elaborates:

> I really wanted to get back into saloon car racing, so I bought a Toyota Celica and entered it in the Monroe Shock Absorber Production Saloon Car Championship, although, as ever, I had to run it on a shoestring budget.

The Bevan/Fraser hybrid.
(Ray Calcutt is at wheel while a crouched George Bevan is checking the tyre pressures).

Although it never made him a rich financially, saloon racing had been good to Ray and the Toyota Celica continued this rewarding tin-top trend. The Celica went wonderfully, netting him the class and third place overall in the Championship against semi-works opposition. In 1984 he also drove a snorting and supremely capable Mitsubishi Colt Starion in the Willhire 24 Hour Race, sharing the car with Andy Maclennan and David Morganin. A good result was in the offing, until the Starion was sidelined by a mechanical problem. Ray continued with his oriental allegiance and in 1985 the Celica made way for a 1.6 Corolla GT and the winning streak continued.

Ray had not quite managed to shake off the Imp bug though and in late 1980s he competed in a Modified Saloon Car Championship in a Hartwell-powered Imp. Ray retired from racing shortly after, although he remains deeply passionate about the sport. He is a member of the BARC; life member of the BRDC, something he is immensely proud of and also belongs to Brighton & Hove Motor Club. Ray spectates at Silverstone on a regular basis and does some vintage and classic car-related work for Bonhams, the auction house.

Bill McGovern — Triple Champion

Bill McGovern is passionate about cars, and is one of those people who were just born to race. The McGovern/Bevan relationship was an enduring one and has become part of saloon car racing's folklore. His giant-slaying acts with the Bevan Imp remain etched in the memory of many an enthusiast's mind. Although his first success came at the wheel of a Mini, his first competitive event was a hillclimb at Woburn Park in 1963 and he was driving a Vauxhall.

> I was using my Vauxhall VX 4/90 at Woburn and despite driving as hard as I could, I was beaten by a Mini Cooper 'S' that had managed to improve on my time by 10 seconds!

Not a man to take such a thing lying down, he soon exchanged the Vauxhall for a Speedwell-tuned Mini 1071 Cooper 'S' and took FTD at a wet Brands Hatch the next weekend. A year later, Bill competed in his first race. He got pole, took 0.2 seconds off the lap record, and finished second overall. Bill's second race was at Snetterton and it was a cracker.

His on-the-limit driving style raised more than a few eyebrows and *Motoring News* was even moved to report:

> The antics of Bill McGovern and Gerry Marshall at the Esses, blanched the faces of even the most hardened spectators.

Bill signed to drive for Paul Emery in 1966, but after a frustrating, although not unhappy period driving the Emery Imp, he went on to drive the Bevan Imp for George Bevan. It was also during this time that he started dabbling with single seaters (he raced as Alan Jones's team-mate in a Brabham BT36 in 1971) and very nearly went into Formula One, but circumstances and common sense prevailed:

I believe I could have been very successful in single seaters. When I started racing I was 26 years old, I was married with four daughters and this fact was always in my mind. Safety was not good back then, and drivers were often getting seriously injured or even killed. I thought it would not be a good idea to end up as an obituary in Autosport.

Indeed, one of Bill's friends, a Formula Ford driver, perceived motor racing as somewhere you would probably die, and as, at this time, McGovern drove every lap on the ragged edge, single seaters were perhaps not the wisest choice for him.

Bill did, however, briefly drive a Dulon Porsche in the BOAC Brands Hatch 1000 km (the engine blew after 1 hour), and also drove a Moskvitch in the Avon Round Britain Tour.

In the BOAC 1000, I managed 9th out of 45, outqualifying a number of notable drivers in the process and was offered a drive at Monaco. Overall though, I concluded that it was too dangerous, the racing circuits at this time had lots of trees and concrete marshals posts and this may have had something to do with my decision.

Bill's decision not to drive single seaters and continue with saloons was good news for tin-top enthusiasts. Bill, George Bevan and, of course, the Bevan Imp, went on to become one of the most successful partnerships ever in British Saloon Car racing history. George and his wife, Doris, looked after Bill well, and Bill remembers his time he spent racing for them with great affection.

Bill was indeed fortunate in that he had one of the best cars in the Championship—and without any doubt, the best car in its class.

George was a brilliant engineer, I do not think that any other Imp has ever been built to the same standard. Quite often I revved it over 10,000 rpm, it delivered superb power and smoothness right across the rev range. George never placed any restrictions on how I drove it—I was always fully confident of the engine's durability. At an event at the Brands Hatch short circuit in 1973, I was able to mix it with the Mustangs and won the race outright.

The Passat could have been good if the right parts had been homologated.

It would be fair to say that Bill was a forceful driver and he used anything he could to gain a psychological advantage over his competitors.

> Even in the pit lane, I always used enormous revs, always a racing start out of the lane. I'd rev the engine up and down-always being as dramatic as I could. Also, I'd make it my business to break the lap record during practice and the warm-up lap, just to shatter their confidence!

Despite rewriting the record books for the previous three years, things did not go well for Bill during the 1973 season. A serious 100 mph accident at Thruxton put him in hospital and wrote off the new car (the impact on the rear of the car was so severe that the engine went under the car, and even his helmet was split). Les Nash went on to win the class in the Championship in Bill's old Imp (he had campaigned a MAE-engined ex-Superspeed Anglia to good effect in previous years).

The 1974 RAC Championship was also notable for its lack of success, as the VW Passat that Bill was using proved to be too heavy and was underpowered because of the homologation problems. The Bevan-modified saloon Imp that Bill raced during the following year was much more successful.

Although he retired from racing at the end of the 1975 season, Bill was tempted back to the circuits in 1978 when he was offered a drive in Michael Holland's 'SIGAS' Bevan Imp. He achieved many class wins and lap records before the car was sold in 1979. George Bevan then built another Imp to BRSCC Modified Saloon Car Championship specification for 1980, and a series of storming drives culminated in Bill winning the Championship outright. Between 1986 and 1989 he raced a Renault 5 GT Turbo with a good degree of success.

Flying in the Modified Saloon Sunbeam Imp.

Bill McGovern retired at the end of the 1989 season to concentrate on running the family business. He was recently tempted to build and race an Imp in one of the historic series, but felt that it would not have been the same without George Bevan around. He is still a keen motorsports enthusiast though, and often attends race meetings up and down the country.

Favourite Circuit(s):

> Brands Hatch closely followed by Cadwell Park.
> You have to be able to drive to do well at these two circuits.

Best Race(s):

> 1972 ADAC Dreilander Tropae, Zandvoort and the 1970 Tourist Trophy.

Memories of George:

> As well as being such an accomplished engineer, George was just such a nice man. Racing with George was an absolute pleasure and a golden period in my life.

Memories of the Bevan Imp:

> What can I say? It was simply a fabulous car that just got better and better. I could drive it as hard as I liked and take all sorts of liberties with it and it simply did everything that was asked of it. The engine was a marvel and the handling was stunning. A brilliant package.

Melvyn Adams — Class Rival

Melvyn Adams has been in love with motor racing since the age of five. Why? Well that is how old he was when his uncle took him to the Easter races at Goodwood, where he remembers being so enthralled by the sights and sounds. One 'notable' driver racing that day in 1952 was a young Stirling Moss in an HWM.

> It was incredible. Even though I was so young, I can still remember how exciting the racing was—and how it affected me. I made up my mind then and there, that someday I would become a racing driver.

Unfortunately for Melvyn, he would have to wait another 17 years until he was able to take to the track himself. When he did, he chose an Imp as his race car.

> I'd been impressed by the performance of Imps in racing, especially the Nathan Imps. There was something quite special and charismatic about these cars, and I decided that an Imp would be the ideal choice of car for me.

Melvyn found that he could not afford to purchase a ready-built racer; he had to look for a much cheaper option and work to an extremely limited budget.

> I went to the local breaker's yard to see if they had any Imps there. Luckily for me, they did have one Imp, but it was a write-off. I bought the Imp and then took it to the local body shop who straightened it out, and I did the rest.

Melvyn's beautifully turned out Imp.

Over a period of a year, Melvyn, with the aid of a few friends, got his £30 acquisition race-ready. The car proved to be successful and Melvyn was quickly on the pace. Indeed, he bagged a lap record at Crystal Palace (a circuit where you could not practise) and won at this circuit again in September. Despite his novice status, his shoestring budget, and being forced to use all second-hand parts, Melvyn managed to end the season a very creditable fourth in the 850 class.

> It was all a bit of a compromise, but despite this, I always made sure that the car was as well prepared and as nicely turned out as it could be.

Suitably buoyed up by his first year's results, Melvyn decided to aim his sights much higher, and in 1970 he entered the British Saloon Car Championship.

> 1970 was a wasted year. I had moved up to the 1-litre class and couldn't really afford it. It wasn't until the end of the year that I started to get some decent results. I tried to enter the 1971 Championship, but couldn't get in. Des O'Dell suggested that somebody who was already a known name in the Championship enter me instead. So, Tony Charnell entered me and I managed to get in. Des had seen that I was going quickly and he was keen to get some more quick Imps in the Championship.

George Bevan was always extremely helpful too and Melvyn found that George was always on hand to help him out. Melvyn ran his Imp using Bevan cast-offs and Peter Bevan used to do the cylinder heads for him. The Adams's Imp, like the Bevan Imp, was an entirely home-built affair. Thompson Engineering did some of the machining, but Melvyn linered the blocks himself and did all the other preparation with the help of a few friends. George built his early engines in his kitchen—but Melvyn was having none of that, he built his in his bedroom! Although Melvyn's Imp went very well, he received little in the way of sponsorship and funded his racing himself. This did not stop him achieving some excellent results and it is to his credit that the car always looked immaculate.

Throughout the 1971 season, Melvyn found that he could beat all the other Imp drivers and set his sights on getting as close to Bill McGovern as possible, and often finished second to the Bevan Imp. At the end of the season Melvyn had done well enough to secure second overall in the class.

The 1972 season went much the same way, and again he finished second to Bill McGovern—but more importantly he was 6th overall in the Championship and won the Privateer's Championship.

In 1973, he finished a tremendous 3rd overall in the Championship. In 1974 Melvyn (who had secured sponsorship from *Cars and Car Conversions* magazine) competed against Bill McGovern once more, this time in a Volkswagen Passat— even managing to beat Bill on one occasion.

Melvyn retired from the sport in the early 1980s. He loved the whole experience and would dearly love to be involved with the cut and thrust of circuit racing once again because he feels that he could still do well. The whole period was a great experience for him and a time he looks back on it with much fondness:

> I had a fantastic time, and my only regret is that I didn't get to drive for George in a professional capacity.

In 1980 Melvyn took to the tracks in a Mark 7a Davrian and raced this as and when he could afford to. Today he supports his son, who races in karts.

Favourite Circuit(s):
Thruxton. I seemed to be able to go well there.

Best Race(s) 1970-80:
1973 RAC round at Thruxton (class win in RAC Championship).
1980 Modsports round at Thruxton.
1974 RAC Round at Silverstone (class win and fastest lap).

Memories of George:
George was a real gentleman and a larger-than-life character, on and off the track—always willing to give advice and he helped me out whenever he could.

Memories of the Bevan Imp:
The Bevan Imp was so well prepared. It had all the best bits on it and Bill was a very rapid driver. I often used to finish second to the Bevan Imp, and towards the end of the 1972 season I was getting closer and closer to it.

Les Nash — Rival and Team-mate

Amongst Les Nash's claims to fame are that he has always been a very quick racing driver and the Ford Anglia he used to compete in was rather garishly hued and dubbed 'The Purple People Eater'! Les was dominant in the Anglia and if he was on the entry list, then the only question on spectator's minds was who would finish second?

From 1967 and right through until 1971 Les drove his ex-Superspeed, MAE-engined Anglia to numerous victories, winning the 1971 Hepolite Glacier Championship outright. Over the years Les steadily developed the Anglia, but

one thing he did not mess around with was its Lucas Engineering-developed MAE engine. The MAE engine is a cracking engine; even in its standard and unmolested form, but to improve its gas flow Lucas did a demon modifica-

Les's infamous Anglia or 'Purple People-Eater'!

tion to the cylinder head. The side ports were blanked off and new ones were drilled from the top of the head. This allowed a pair of menacing Porsche downdraught Webers to be fitted and the net result of all this handiwork was an impressive 123 bhp at the flywheel and oodles of torque.

Les had an impressive race car, but he could not have managed to race it at all, had it not been for the support of his younger brother, Colin, who attended and helped out at every race meeting in the early years.

Unfortunately, the ferociously quick Anglia was written off in 1971 sidelining Les so in 1972 he took time out to concentrate on his business and consolidate funds. Keen to get back on the track in 1973, Les was contemplating what car to buy, when he heard that the triple Championship-winning Imp was up for grabs.

> I heard through the grapevine that the Bevan Imp was up for sale. I thought that this car might provide a rather good route back into racing and it was perfect for the RAC series.

Having had three competitive years at the front of the pack the car was a little tired but on the whole it was still in good condition. After meeting with George and agreeing terms, Les bought the car although there were certain conditions attached to the sale:

> I agreed to the price and told George I would do the general maintenance. George insisted that he would do all the engines and if there were any problems at race meetings, then he'd do the repairs for free. Between us we also agreed that we would run the old car and Bill's new Sunbeam Imp as a team.

Les, who did not want to upset what could have been a fourth Championship-winning year, offered to play second fiddle to Bill. As it transpired, due to circumstances and mechanical issues, Les never ever had to obey 'team orders'.

Unlike Bill's first race with the Imp at Brands back in 1970, which was blighted by mechanical problems, Les's 1973 Imp début was rather more successful—although the practice session was an unusually fraught affair.

> The engine played up during practice, but I just managed to get the mandatory three laps in. George and his team changed the engine for the race but because of the problems I found myself at the back of the grid.

Having had a year away from the racing scene, Les was a little anxious. After all, he was driving a new car with a different engine configuration to the Anglia. If that was not enough to contend with, due to the practice problems, he would have to fight his way through from the back of the grid. Bill McGovern, as irrepressible as ever, put Les's mind at rest.

> Bill said not to worry as he would hold the field up (in this up-to-1300 race) as I manoeuvred my way through the pack.

True to his word, Bill comfortably assumed a leading role and was soon way out in front. Bill 'blocked' the rest of the competition and Les took the 'old' Bevan Imp by the scruff of the neck, powered his way through to second place. Bill, who by now was some way in front, was on his way to what should have been a comfortable win, had some mechanical maladies and pitted. Les, some way behind, was not aware of this fact and just assumed that Bill was miles ahead:

> I couldn't see the other Imp, so I assumed (wrongly) that Bill must have been flying. I was rather disillusioned, thinking that I was so far behind Bill, so I drove as hard as I could to catch up. You can imagine my surprise when I crossed the finishing line in first place!

At Silverstone Bill and Les were pretty evenly matched with Les slip-streaming Bill lap after lap. At Woodcote Corner, Les was a touch quicker than Bill and ran right alongside him at the line with Bill just taking the win. There was a method in Les's last-minute dash though.

> People thought I was trying to beat Bill. In fact, I didn't want to, I just wanted it to be known that I was as quick as him!

It did not take Les too long to acclimatise to his new steed. The Bevan Imp handled nicely, it had a good power output and the lap times were around the same as the Anglia, it was just the brakes that caught him out from time-to-time.

> The Imp seemed to lock the back wheels rather too easily. If I used the engine as a brake then dropped down two gears for a corner, then when I braked the wheels would lock up. I got used to this characteristic in the end though.

The 'old' Bevan Imp had now become the 'new' Purple People-Eater! Les at Brands in October 1973.

1973 was far from a vintage year for the Bevan team as both cars (especially Bill's new Sunbeam Imp) suffered from a rash of component failures. Bill also had a horrendous crash at Thruxton (not through any fault of his own it should be added), which hospitalised him and effectively wrote off his season too.

> Bill used to win the class when I broke down and I used to win the class when he broke down. I can't actually remember us finishing a race together apart from at Silverstone.

Les did, however, manage to finish enough races and accumulate enough points to achieve an excellent class title and fourth place overall.

With new regulations looming for 1974, Les decided to sell the Imp and invest in a completely different type of car.

> I sold the Imp back to George at the end of the season and I think George sold the car on to someone in Belgium. I decided to race a Camaro because I had a business that dealt with American cars. Initially the RAC were going to allow cars like the Camaro/Trans Am to compete, but when the RAC decided to go Group 1 they determined they were not eligible.

Les, who had spent a lot of time and money preparing the car, then had to sell it. Later in the day the RAC changed its mind and allowed in the 'muscle' cars. Les was forced to buy another Camaro, but it was all done in haste and his new acquisition proved to be no more than a heap of junk.

> The second Camaro was a disaster. I spent loads of money trying to improve it and the project nearly bankrupted me!

Still, Les had done enough to impress and Bill Shaw Racing offered him a works-supported drive. But Les was not keen on using a Dolomite Sprint; he still hankered after a competitive Camaro. No deal could be brokered, so Les went his own way, eventually retiring from the sport in 1976. He did not race again until 1986 when the resurgence in interest in historic racing lured him back to the race tracks. Les campaigned a Lotus Cortina in 1986 and still races one with great success.

> I really enjoy the historic racing scene and will continue to race for as long as I can.

Favourite Circuit(s)
> Brands Hatch Grand Prix Circuit and Cadwell Park.

Best Race(s) 1970-80
> I enjoyed them all when I was fortunate to finish.

Memories of George
> George Bevan was an extremely likeable man. His wife gave him full support with his racing. Both were genuine people whom I admired and respected immensely.

Memories of the Bevan Imp
> Would like to know if the old girl still exists?

Richard Longman — The Mini Maestro

Working as a mechanic at Downton Engineering, it was inevitable that Richard Longman's life would become inextricably bound up with the world of motor sport and the Mini. Richard Longman was one of the quickest of Mini drivers and he would become one of the country's foremost and best regarded of tuners. If you can drive a Mini well, you are part-way there. If that Mini happens to have a Longman engine then it is guaranteed to be a front-runner.

Richard's first forays into motor racing were not behind the wheel, but under the bonnet, as he wielded the spanners for friend and fellow Downton employee Barry Hawkins (the pair had built a race Mini together). After a season helping out on this car, Richard decided that it was high time that he had a go behind the wheel himself.

His first race, in 1966, was at Llandow and he acquitted himself very well. Richard was well and truly bitten by the racing bug and he raced, hillclimbed and sprinted his self-prepared 850 Mini (for which, Downton's chief, Daniel Richmond provided the parts) whenever the opportunity arose. By 1968, the car's engine had grown to 1300 cc and Richard had moved to pastures new.

I was offered a very good position at Janspeed. Janspeed were relatively new to the performance-tuning scene, and very keen to promote their range of tuning accessories.I provided the car, and they supplied me with everything necessary to ensure that the Janspeed equipped Mini was a consistent front-runner.

Richard Longman steering his 1293 Mini to the front.

Not one to be easily intimidated, Richard forces his way alongside Martin Birrane's Falcon.

Downton in the meantime had kept an eye on their former employee's achievements. Liking what they saw, they headhunted Richard in 1969, offering a better salary and, the icing on the cake as far as he was concerned, an ex-Britax Group 5 Mini Cooper S. Richard and his new steed achieved many podium places, the highpoints of the season being the Race of Champions win at Brands Hatch and the BBC Grandstand Trophy win at Thruxton. Commentating on the Thruxton race was no other than a certain Graham Hill. Hill, having made references to the fact that Richard's Mini would soon drop down the running order, was forced to eat humble pie when Richard managed to not only keep up the pace, but to also pass the Broadspeed Escorts, Ford Falcons 'et al' and go on to win the race!

Indeed, 1969 was a vintage year for Richard for he was Britain's most successful racing driver having won 27 out of 36 races entered.

> Looking back on this period, I wonder how I ever found the time or the energy to compete in so many races!

With these impressive performances under his belt and a growing reputation as a very capable driver, it was inevitable that Richard and his Mini would soon be making the transition from club racing tussles to national championship battles. In April 1970, Richard joined the other hopefuls on the grid at Brands Hatch, ready to throw down the gauntlet to whomsoever would pick it up. Richard was soon on the pace and race-by-race he steadily climbed up the points table. Unfortunately, brake problems at Silverstone during Round 6 caused his and the Mini's premature departure from the race, and from the Championship. The car was written-off in the accident and front-runner Richard found himself relegated to the sidelines, and his car consigned to the scrap heap. Downton seemingly lost heart and in a somewhat surprising, and certainly disappointing move (as far as Richard was concerned) they decided not to rebuild the car and withdrew from the series.

By 1971 Richard felt that he no longer had a future at Downton, so he left to set up in business on his own. His first project was to build a new car for the RAC series and then find a driver to pilot it.

> I wanted someone else to drive the car and win with it. Then everyone would know it was my engines that were winning, not me!

Jonathan Buncombe was the driver he chose and Jonathan and the Longman Mini went on to notch up some extremely impressive results and showcased Richard's fledgling company very well.

In 1972 Richard was offered a Formula 3 drive and he jumped at the opportunity to get behind the wheel once more. He very swiftly acclimatised to single seaters, getting pole position at Silverstone and beating the likes of Alan Jones, Jody Scheckter and James Hunt. His exploits did not go unnoticed, and March Engineering thought enough of his ability behind the wheel to offer him a drive. But Richard's new company was doing well and he was forced to make the decision whether to concentrate on his business or try to make it as a top-flight driver.

He chose the former. Richard did not vacate the driving seat for long though. He occasionally raced Minis in club events, and by the late 'seventies his company was doing sufficiently well that he was able to enter the RAC Championship once again, but this time using the Mini 1275 GT. Richard came 5th in 1977 and went on to win the Championship in 1978 and 1979 and came very close to winning in the early 1980s in a Metro. Richard has also raced successfully abroad, in Europe and in South America.

Over the years, Richard Longman Racing has become synonymous with top quality engineering and, of course, the Mini. Other marques have also benefited from the Longman touch, particularly those with a Peugeot badge. Longman prepared Peugeot 306s won the Asia Touring Car Championship in 2000, 2001 and 2002. Richard Longman continues to head the successful company he established some thirty-two years ago and despite the tremendous variety of modern and hi-tech cars that pass through the doors of his workshop, he will always be known as the Mini 'maestro'.

Favourite Circuit(s)
> Thruxton. I felt that if you could go quickly here, you go quickly anywhere.

Best Race(s) 1970-80
> 1969 Race of Champions.

Memories of George
> George and his whole team were very friendly people.

Memories of the Bevan Imp
> It was a very well prepared car and was extremely quick. At circuits such as Brands Hatch and Mallory Park, it was virtually unbeatable.

Jonathan Buncombe — Mini Ace

With a father who was a works HRG driver, and a mother who used to compete in numerous and varied motorsports events, it was inevitable that Jonathan Buncombe would follow in their footsteps. And, how many people can say that their first track outing was a British Grand Prix support race? Well, Jonathan can. Back in 1955, he came home a highly respectable 5th—albeit in a pedal car race!

Although hugely successful in Capris, Jonathan is remembered for the most part because of his giant-killing exploits in various Minis. After a period racing karts, Jonathan moved into saloon cars using a Mini. This first Mini was a rough car, registration 469 BOF, which his mother had taken in as a part-exchange (she ran a business that specialised in Minis) and apprentice mechanic, Jonathan, did all the preparation himself. His first event in the car was at the 1965 Holly Marine Sprint organised by the Burnham-on-Sea Motor Club and, using his 930 Mini, he won his class.

> My father and mother established the Burnham-on-Sea Motor Club, which in the 'sixties was a huge motor club, one of the biggest in the UK.

Although he prepared the cars himself (and to an extremely high standard), Jonathan was shrewd enough to appreciate that no matter how quick you were, you could only achieve good results if you had a powerful and reliable engine.

From day one he invested in only the best, namely Downton engines. At the time, Downton Engineering produced the finest BMC engines around. Jonathan's friend, Richard Longman, was then working at Downton and also competed with a Mini (although he was in a different class). They used to talk often about moving from sprints, hillclimbs and autocross (Jonathan also autocrossed a Cooper 'S') to circuit racing. Richard took the plunge, but Jonathan felt that he was not yet brave enough to take to the circuits. However, with a bit of persuasion, he soon followed suit and entered a race at Llandow in May 1967.

> It was a wet race, and the bigger-engined cars were at a bit of a disadvantage. Much to my surprise, and bearing in mind that this was my first race, I found that I was able to drive around them on the corners and pull away to win the race.

Jonathan and his new Mini really 'clicked.'

A few days later, at Castle Coombe, he was in the lead again and miles ahead of the opposition when, with only two laps to go, he ran out of fuel! This was a great disappointment, but one that Jonathan put down to being part of the learning curve, and from then on he set his sights on doing as well as possible—and always ensuring he had enough petrol in the tank!

By 1968, and funding his racing almost entirely on his apprentice's wages, he had managed over twenty-odd second places, finishing right on the tail of the flying Richard Longman. As a schoolboy, Jonathan had admired the exploits of drivers of the calibre of Chris Craft and John Fitzpatrick. His dream was to be able to emulate them by competing in the 1300 class in the RAC Championship. It would not be too long, before Jonathan would do more than emulate them, he would soon find himself competing against them and leading them home.

Jonathan's mother really encouraged him and helped too. Seeing that he was doing so well and that his budget was so tight, she presented him with a brand new Mini Cooper which Jonathan converted to full Cooper 'S' specification complete with a full-race Downton 1293 cc unit.

In a way my mother was more of a petrolhead than my father!

The jump from 930 to 1293 cc surprised Jonathan. The larger engine produced a lot more torque than the peaky 930, and made the car much easier to drive.

Suitably encouraged, he entered the RAC Championship in 1969 and set his mind on becoming the highest placed privateer. A string of good results, many seventh overalls, the occasional sixth, and one stunning second place at Thruxton boded well for his future, if not for his car. The RAC Championship rounds plus numerous club events had taken their toll on the Mini; it had also been reshelled due to a crash. Jonathan decided that it was time to part with the car and he sold it to an American buyer for £1,500 (the car is still competing Stateside today, and does well in historic events).

For 1970 a change of vehicle was felt to be a good move, and Jonathan purchased a left-hand-drive, Solex-carbureted, BMW 2002 Ti. Unfortunately, whilst the BMW was able to win club events, it was not able to touch an Escort in the national Championship, because it was underpowered and far too heavy. Discouraged with its lacklustre performance and engine problems, he tried to sell the car, but no one was interested and the BMW remained with him for some time. It seemed that both Jonathan and the car were going nowhere in 1970.

Thankfully, every cloud has a silver lining and for Jonathan, it came in the shape of Richard Longman Racing. During the winter of 1970, Richard Longman had left Downton Engineering to set up his own business, but he had also been contracted to drive a Formula Three car and needed someone to promote his fledgling business.

Richard contacted me, and said that if I could build a rolling shell, he would provide the engine and gearbox.

The BMW was very successful on the club scene but outpaced at national level.

Jonathan built a car and entered the Osram/GEC Club Championship in 1970 using a Longman engine built by Richard Longman's partners, George Toath and Steve Harris. George fettled the head, and Steve who worked in the experimental engine department built the engine. Steve also travelled to every race with Jonathan and kept an eagle eye on the engine. The Buncombe/Longman partnership was extremely successful, winning every race bar one (when the throttle cable broke) and took the Championship title in fine style.

At the end of the 1971 season, Jonathan converted the Mini to Group 2 specification in readiness to tackle the RAC Championship, although not everyone shared his enthusiasm for the Mini. By 1972, the general consensus of opinion was that (in the RAC Championship anyway), the car was outdated and no longer on the pace. However, Jonathan and Richard felt otherwise and set out to prove that a properly developed Mini was still a winner. At the heart of the Richard Longman Racing Mini, was a super RLR engine, built to slay giants.

Steve built a brilliant engine, it was his baby, and the car was really on the pace.

Despite what the pundits had thought and said pre-season, Jonathan proved them wrong, notching up a number of class and race wins (up-to-1300 cc) on his way to securing the class title and a magnificent fourth overall in the Championship.

Although racing is a costly exercise, Jonathan found that if you were doing well, then racing at national level was more cost-effective than doing club events. By virtue of good overall and class placings, he accrued quite a lot of prize money (sometimes up to £1000 per race). With free tyres from Dunlop (Jonathan used to undertake tyre testing for them) free oil, free shock absorbers, free spark plugs and other handouts from manufacturers, he managed to end the season with cash in hand.

A mechanically sympathetic driver, Jonathan had other attributes so important to racing success, a keen hearing and a good sense of smell!

> I always kept an ear on the engine to listen to how healthy everything was, and I also developed my sense of smell, just in case there were any oil leaks or similar which needed a quick investigative pit stop.

Despite the hectic saloon car schedule, Jonathan and his father found time to trial an ex-works Rallye Imp, one that reputedly used to belong to Rosemary Smith. The duo were also responsible for the fearsome Chevron-chassied and BDA-powered 'Chimp,' which provided Jonathan with many Special Saloon Car race wins.

Nowadays, Jonathan has retired from the motor trade, and among other things he supports his sons' hugely successful racing exploits. When possible, he also finds the time to race a rather nice Lotus Cortina in European FIA Historic races; although he is still rather surprised that no one has ever asked him to race a Mini in such events.

Favourite Circuit(s)
> Cadwell Park and Crystal Palace—These were real drivers' circuits and had a terrific ambience.

Memories of George
> George was a real gentleman. It was a pleasure to have known him. Everyone liked him.

Memories of the Bevan Imp
> Nothing significant really, but it was really well-prepared, quick for a 1-litre too, but I can't ever remember seeing it in my mirror. It didn't cause me any trouble that I can recall.

Vince Woodman — Blue Oval Racer

Cars have been the focus of Vince Woodman's life since a very early age. So much so, in fact, that he started his own garage business in 1961 and just two years later he began a long term and highly successful partnership with the Ford Motor Company. Vince was a consistent pace maker in the Escorts and had it not been for a catalogue of mechanical problems, then he too, could have been a Championship winner.

Despite his involvement with Ford, Vince's first proper road car was a Triumph TR3. It was not long before this roadgoing TR3 began to be used in anger and

Vince Woodman.

Vince made the transition from spectator to competitor.

I was a member of the Bristol Motorcycle and Light Car Club. I went to watch a hillclimb at Durham Park, and seeing as they were low on entries I decided to step into the breach and have a go. Thus started my competition career!

Vince was smitten and by 1964 he and the TR3 were regulars on the Castle Coombe and Mallory Park sprint scene. The need for speed resulted in the TR3 being replaced by an altogether more powerful steed, the ex-Gibson Jarvey Jaguar E-type, registration number UDT 100. Vince was doing a lot of business with UDT at the time and this was reflected in the price he paid for the car—a mere £1,200!

Vince's motorsports activities and the success he was having, had not gone unnoticed by Ford, prompting them to question him why—as he was a Ford dealer—was he using a Jaguar? This observation came at an opportune moment for Vince, as the Jaguar, although highly modified, was still too heavy and he had been considering replacing it. Unfortunately, Ford's interest did not manifest itself in the form of a free 'works' car. However, Vince took the corporate 'hint' and went and bought himself a Lotus Cortina Mark 1 and at the same time Vince moved away from the hills and on to the circuits.

A smooth and consistently quick driver—especially in the wet—he was quickly on the pace with the Cortina. Ford, ever watchful, appreciated this move and they soon rewarded him for his efforts and his brand loyalty.

I did very well with the Lotus Cortina, and one of the highlights of my time with it was when I beat Roger Clark at Mallory Park. It was because of this that I got my Ford contract.

By 1970 Vince Woodman Motors had moved up in the world, becoming Ford main dealers (Vince became the youngest proprietor of a Ford main dealership in the country) and his relationship with the factory really began to blossom.

Ford desperately wanted an Escort to win the RAC Saloon Car Championship with, and in 1970 they gave the contract to prepare the works cars to Broadspeed (a few years earlier Broadspeed had run a brace of 1-litre Anglias in minor championships with Ford backing. In 1968 they had fielded the new Escort and narrowly missed securing the Championship title in 1969). Vince, who had run a Broadspeed customer car in 1969, once more, joined Chris Craft and John Fitzpatrick on the grid to head up a very talented Escort assault on the Championship. Vince was no stranger to the Anglia's replacement, as in 1968 he had driven a development Escort on a number of occasions—even winning a race at Thruxton in it.

Although Broadspeed prepared Vince's new mount, he ran the Escort himself, using his own team of people, but in conjunction with Broadspeed and under the Ford banner.

The Escort initially had a terrific 1-litre twin-cam engine, and was a very special car. It produced a lot of power, but the car was really too heavy for such a small unit, and unfortunately this potentially very lively engine also suffered from a lack of development. The ensuing reliability problems prompted us to install a 1300 cc unit and move up a class, which, in many ways, was a shame.

It took a while for Broadspeed to sort out the Escort's handling!

179

Ford's new family saloon was already making a name for itself as a forest tiger, but it took some time before the car really tamed the circuits. The regulations regarding suspension had been tightened up but in the paddock many variations on the Escort suspension theme could still be found. Every team had their own ideas of how the Escort's suspension should be developed. Vince found that his Escort lifted a front wheel—even higher than an Imp—and understeered dramatically at the same time. Ralph Broad was a superb engineer and he master-minded the development programme and his team worked hard to perk up the Escort's on-track handling. When the roll centre was lowered and the rear track widened, the Broadspeed Escorts really began to corner with aplomb and the cars became much more competitive.

Vince went on to drive 1300, 1600, and 2-litre Escorts in the Championship. In 1973, despite winning a total of 22 races in Europe and the UK, the RAC Championship title still eluded him. Vince also raced Escorts and Capris in selected ETC races at circuits such as Paul Ricard and Spa.

Like others who competed in the RAC Championship during this halcyon period, Vince fondly remembers the time as being a wonderful episode in his life.

> Back then, there were a super lot of people involved with the touring cars and the cars were not too far removed from what you could see in the showroom.

Nowadays, Vince is still involved with the garage trade and runs VMW Motors near Bristol, which specialises in low mileage, as new, cars. He still has Ford blood in his veins though. Tucked safely away from prying eyes is his pride and joy, a full-house Cologne Capri. He has not forsaken the track either. Vince is a chief instructor for the Ferrari Owners' Club and was an occasional competitor in the club's 2002 Pirelli Maranello Ferrari Challenge.

Favourite Circuit(s)

> Mallory Park was one of my favourites and of course my local circuit Castle Coombe has always a great place to compete.

Best Race(s) 1970-80

> 1973 Hilton Trophy at Crystal Palace, 1973 ETC 24 Hour Nivelles race (with Andy Rouse).

Memories of George

> George was a great bloke. Despite the intense competition, everyone in the Bevan team was always polite and helpful. It was a super time in my life and one that I look back upon with great affection.

Memories of the Bevan Imp

> I enjoyed competing against the Imp immensely. It was a really quick car, immaculately turned out and beautifully prepared.

David Matthews — Close Competition

David Matthews is one of a handful of drivers who truly deserved to win the British Saloon Car Championship. The fact that he did not win the coveted title was down to the scoring structure, of points being available equally in all four engine sized classes. The super reliable, quick and well-driven Bevan Imp won the title both years when David was runner-up overall.

Although David's career was cut short by a racing accident in 1973, he remains to this day passionate about the sport and is a founding partner with John Booth in Manor Motorsport—the Yorkshire-based team best known for competing in Formula 3 and Formula Renault.

Like many of his contemporaries, David's racing career began behind the wheel of a Mini; it was a home-built machine, which he worked on during evenings and week-ends. It also had quite an interesting history.

David Matthews

I paid £30 for this Mini, it had been written off against a Derbyshire wall. Luckily it was an early model and sometime later I discovered that the early cars were built lighter by about 40 lbs, which was, of course, handy for racing.

Apprentice mechanic, David, knocked the Mini into shape and then campaigned it on northern race circuits. After cutting his teeth with the Mini, David was keen to get higher up the grid, so in 1969 he switched to club-racing a rather special ex-Alan Mann Racing Group 5 1600 Escort. This car had previously been campaigned by no less a luminary than Frank Gardner and was owned by entrepreneur, Kevin Macdonald, and raced under the banner of Melton Racing. It was a supremely quick car and in David's talented hands it continued its winning ways.

In 1970, David began racing two cars—one for club and one for internationals. Joining the Group 5 Escort was an ex-John Fitzpatrick 1300 cc Broadspeed car, built for international Group 2. Excellent results were achieved in this car (once beating all the 1600 cc twin-cams at Cadwell), which got David noticed and in 1971 Ralph Broad approached him with the offer of a supported drive in the British Saloon Car Championship. David and Kevin McDonald jumped at the opportunity and with a new car won the 1300 cc category in the Championship at the first attempt, with numbers of poles, fastest laps and lap records. In fact, they were winning the actual Championship 'overall' until the very last race at Brands when their engine broke—and Bill McGovern, yet again, took the Championship.

I remember being very, very, very sad at the time!

For 1972, David was picked-up professionally by Stuart Turner and the Ford Motor Company who provided him with two cars, spares plus a transporter. The first car for internationals was an Escort BDA 1800 cc bored out to 2000 cc from a thick-wall block. The motor delivered more than 265 bhp working in a very light car. The second car was a 3-litre Capri for the new National Group 1 and Broadspeed prepared both cars at David's request.

Racing hard through the year David started 34 times and won the race or his class on 26 occasions—despite which he still finished second overall in both Championships—such was the quality of competition in touring car racing in the early 1970s. Again, Bill McGovern took honours overall in the international category, being superbly reliable, very quick, and very consistent throughout.

Of all the drivers whom he competed against, David cites Dave Brodie as being a hard man to beat—and Frank Gardner as being the man he would have most liked to beat.

Although Frank was driving that big Camaro, the 2-litre 265 bhp lightweight BDA Escort was really quick in its final evolution and I could have nailed Frank on several occasions, particularly as during the longer races the Camaro used to heat up and run out of brakes and clutch.

David Matthews—sideways to victory and to recognition.

International pacesetter.

On one occasion at Brands, the Camaro was leaking oil and was beginning to burn underneath. David, who had a real chance to overtake was unable to do so because of lack of visibility—his Escort's windscreen was awash with the Camaro's oil. The marshals should have pulled Gardner into the pits, but did not and David had no choice other than to sit on the Camaro's tail and win his class. But for the Camaro's smoke screen he might well have won the race. On other occasions his attempts to slip past the Camaro would be rewarded with a knock—there were several occasions when the Broadspeed Escort ended a race with a Camaro-shaped dent in its door! Keeping up with Frank Gardner was one thing, getting past him was another. David had him dead to rights at Crystal Palace in the wet but the Camaro came back into the Escort's radiator. David said later:

> You learn a lot racing against Frank.

Like the majority of those who competed during this period, David recalls it also as being a happy, if somewhat frenetic time.

> The grids were huge and the racing was close. In the bigger-engined classes you had to win all the rounds to beat the ultra-reliable 1-litre Bevan Imp, which won pretty much every time out. The larger classes were packed with strong competitors and numbers of drivers would have liked an extra point or two for the stronger competition.

For 1973 David was offered by Ford to drive a factory Broadspeed 3-litre V6 Cologne Capri in Group 2, although the arrival of Group 1 meant that interest in the British International Championship was beginning to wane. David's career was cut short at the British Grand Prix support race at Silverstone in August. Having just lapped Gavin Booth's 1-litre Mini, Booth tried to slipstream the Capri and the Mini clipped one of the Capri's rear wheels knocking David off the track and the Capri became airborne at about 130 mph. Following the ensuing impacts, David's heart was stopped by the shock and ultimately he lost most of the sight in his left eye although he would eventually make a full recovery.

> The medical people were standing on the corner and saved my bacon.

On the other hand Brodie, who was almost right behind and having a ding-dong battle with Andy Rouse, had nowhere to go and hit Booth's Mini—in the subsequent accident Gavin Booth was severely injured (sadly he would lose his life some time later). Brodie's Escort flipped high in the air and burst into flames. Dave Brodie suffered serious leg injuries and although he too would recover, the accident kept him away from racing for two years. All in all, it was a black day for saloon car racing. The authorities were swift to act and introduced the 107 per cent qualifying rule to avoid such a disparity in speed, in future, between the various sized classes of cars competing.

Later, and off the circuits, David went on to build up a successful motor business that became Plaxton Group Plc.

His son, James, raced karts and became British Junior Champion—then on to Formula Renault with John Booth at Manor Motorsport, where James won both European and UK Championships in 1999, equalling Alain Prost's all time series win record of 11 wins from 13 races.

In more recent years, David has worked in this country and overseas as an investor. He has financial and property interests and also owns the Eden Rock in St. Barths in the French West Indies.

Favourite Circuit(s)

> All of them!

Best Race(s) 1970-80

> 1969-1973 —Loved all of them, but really enjoyed winning the knock-about Celebrity Race at Brands in 1972 as part of the International Meeting. 3-litre Capri's were used and Graham Hill was second, Dave Brodie third, and Howden Ganley was fourth.

Memories of George

> George was a lovely chap, professional, friendly and approachable.

Memories of the Bevan Imp

> The Bevan Imp was a very successful Championship winning car.
> Reliability from George and quick as you like from Bill McGovern both in the wet and dry.

CHAPTER **12**

Mechanic's tale

B
EVAN team mechanic Royston Paskins worked for George in a full time
capacity between 1971 and 1973 (although there was a short spell when
the two parted company after a disagreement). A few years earlier
Royston had worked for George in a voluntary capacity.

> I was working for Crippspeed and mad about motor racing and in the mid-1960s.
> I used to help Ken Costello (the man responsible for the Costello MGB V8) with
> his race Mini. At this time, Peter Bevan and Ginger Payne were racing the A40s.
> Ginger was very hard on the gearboxes and I used to help George rebuild the
> gearboxes and get parts for him.

Royston was really keen to work for George but it was actually Peter who took him
under his wing initially.

> Peter was working at Pipers at the time and I went to work for Peter, thinking that
> this would be a good way of getting to work for George. When Peter left Pipers
> and began working for himself, I went with him.

Royston did get the chance to work for George in 1971, after his previous
mechanic, Keith Tilbrook, was seriously injured in a road accident. Keith only
made a partial recovery and was unable to work to the same level as he had done
previously.

Working with George was rewarding, although Royston did discover that he
was an extremely hard taskmaster.

> He was a really nice man, but he wanted his pound of flesh from those who
> worked for him. There was one time when I asked for permission to go to a
> wedding but George refused, just in case I didn't turn up for the race the next day.
> My daughter, Georgina, even celebrated her first birthday at Silverstone Circuit,
> such was the commitment George required!
>
> George and I got on well though most of the time and he would do anything for
> anybody.

If working for George proved difficult on occasions, it was rewarding and working with the Imp proved to be a revelation to Royston and he loved the Imp's all-aluminium engine.

> I had been brought up with all the rumours and tales of dread about the Imp engine, but it really is a superb unit. Once you'd learned your way around it and knew how to treat it properly, it is a brilliant engine. I was punch drunk on the Imp engine and used to find any excuse to strip one down and then titivate or rebuild it!

Although Royston and George parted company during 1973, he did come back to work for George later that year as George was fielding the old Bevan Imp for Les Nash and the new twin-headlight Sunbeam Imp Sport for Bill McGovern. In 1974 Royston began working for Baldyne Engineering.

Today, Royston works as an engine builder at Caterham Cars.

Not forgotten.

Champion Roll Call

1958	Jack Sears	Austin A105
1959	Jeff Uren	Ford Zephyr
1960	Doc Shepherd	Austin A40
1961	Sir John Whitmore	Austin Mini
1962	John Love	Mini Cooper
1963	Jack Sears	Ford Cortina GT/Lotus Cortina/Galaxie
1964	Jim Clark	Ford Lotus Cortina
1965	Roy Pierpoint	Ford Mustang
1966	John Fitzpatrick	Ford Anglia
1967	Frank Gardner	Ford Falcon
1968	Frank Gardner	Ford Cortina/Anglia
1969	Alec Poole	Mini Cooper 'S'
1970	**Bill McGovern**	**Sunbeam Imp**
1971	**Bill McGovern**	**Sunbeam Imp**
1972	**Bill McGovern**	**Sunbeam Imp**
1973	Frank Gardner	Chevrolet Camaro
1974	Bernard Unett	Hillman Avenger
1975	Andy Rouse	Dolomite Sprint
1976	Bernard Unett	Chrysler Avenger
1977	Bernard Unett	Chrysler Avenger
1978	Richard Longman	Mini 1275GT
1979	Richard Longman	Mini 1275GT

1980	Win Percy	Mazda RX7
1981	Win Percy	Mazda RX7
1982	Win Percy	Toyota Corolla
1983	Andy Rouse	Alfa Romeo GTV6
1984	Andy Rouse	Rover Vitesse
1985	Andy Rouse	Ford Sierra Turbo
1986	Chris Hodgetts	Toyota Corolla
1987	Chris Hodgetts	Toyota Corolla
1988	Frank Syntner	BMW M3
1989	John Cleland	Vauxhall Astra
1990	Rob Gravett	Ford Sierra RS500
1991	Will Hoy	BMW M3
1992	Tim Harvey	BMW 318i
1993	Jo Wincklehock	BMW 320i
1994	Gabrielle Tarquini	Alfa Romeo 155
1995	John Cleland	Vauxhall Cavalier
1996	Frank Biela	Audi A4 Quattro
1997	Alan Menu	Renault Laguna
1998	Rickard Rydell	Volvo S40
1999	Laurence Aiello	Nissan Primera
2000	Alain Menu	Ford Mondeo
2001	Jason Plato	Vauxhall Astra Coupé
2002	James Thompson	Vauxhall Astra Coupé
2003	Yvan Muller	Vauxhall Astra Coupé

Jack Sears on his way to the 1958 title.

Yvan Muller takes the 2003 title.

188

Index

Index

Jones, Alan 161, 172

K
Kemilainen, Heikei 104
Kent Messenger 160
Kervinen, Ukko 140-141
Knight, Jack 51, 76
Kofoed, Jorgen 94
Kynsilehto, Juhani 35, 86, 135-139, 141

L
Land Rover 9
Lanfranchi, Tony 129
Le Mans 150
Lenham GT 158
Lepistö, Veikko 137, 141
Lister-Bristol 147
Longman, Richard 68, 99, 170-176
Lotus 16, 19, 23, 76, 104, 148, 150, 158, 177-178
Lund, Paul 94
Lynton 80

M
Macdonald, Kevin 181
Maclennan, Andy 161
Mallory Park 93, 110, 178
Manor Motorsport 181
March Engineering 172
Marshall, Gerry 69-70, 73-74, 150
Martino Finotto 90
Martish, Jamika 121
Martish, Jaroslav 121
Mason, Rob 35, 110,
Matthews, David 84, 93, 98, 103-104, 181-182
Matthews, Fred 34
Mazda 68
McKee, Ken 150
McLaren M18 160
Meads, S. J. 30
Melton Racing 181
Mendham, Mo 81, 98, 101
MG 147, 150
Mini 13, 33, 57-58, 63, 68, 102, 108, 110, 132, 170-172, 175-176, 181

Minilite 49
Mitsubishi 161
Mohr, Manfred 109
Montague, Chris 102, 110
Moore, Don 13
Morgan 147
Morganin, David 161
Morris Minor 9
Moskvitch 162
Moss, Stirling 11, 164
Motor 78
Motoring News 158
Mountains Garage 23, 155, 158
Mowatt, Bill 92
Muir, Brian 74, 90, 92

N
Nash, Colin 167
Nash, Les 96, 163, 167-170, 186
Needell, Tiff 150
Nightingale, Jeremy 65, 75

O
O'Dell, Des 71, 80, 84, 125-127, 132-133, 165
Oliver, Jackie 33
Oulton Park 18, 76, 82, 92, 100, 107, 132

P
Paskins, Georgina 185
Paskins, Royston 80, 98, 119, 185-186
Payne, Ginger 32, 185
Payne, Ray 134
Peacock, Brian 87
Peugeot 125
Pierpoint, Roy 19
Piper 31, 185
Pirelli World Rallying 136
Plaxton Group Plc 184
Porsche 162
Practical Motorist 160
Pritchard-Lovell, Brian 22
Prost, Alain 184

R
RAC 57, 68, 71, 79, 83, 88, 92, 98, 120, 167-169, 172, 175-176